50 Years
of
Plowing
Planting
and
Watering

Life Story of

B. R. LAKIN

By Wm. K. "Kenny" McComas

Printed In The United States of America By
DANIELS PUBLISHERS
1209 29th Street
Orlando, Florida 32805

DEDICATION

This book is "affectionately" dedicated to Mrs. Lakin, the "Unsung Hero" of Dr. Lakin's life. If I may be permitted to coin a phrase from the Wise Man Solomon, who in his efforts to describe the ideal woman said, "Her price is far above rubies. Her children rise up and call her blessed; her husband also, and he *praiseth her.*" While her husband for over half a Century was on the Front Line of Battle, she stood faithfully by the "stuff" at home. She maintained a place of refuge for her "Soldier Of The Cross" husband to flee when he became battle-fatigued. Mrs. Lakin's crown will be star-studded for her part in every precious soul her husband won to Christ. She will shine through Eternity as the firmament and as the stars forever and ever.

Wm. K. McComas

TABLE OF CONTENTS

INTRODUCTION

The record of unusual lives must not be lost to the generations yet to come. There has not been a more unusual Christian life in this generation than that of Dr. B. R. Lakin. Through this man God has demonstrated His great power and has shown to the human race once again what one life can mean to the world.

This man of God has passed over the face of the earth for more than half a century, preaching constantly the Word of God and its message of life to unnumbered multitudes. No man can give of himself so long and so intensely, without learning much in the laboratory of human experience. Not only has B. R. Lakin had his soul and body forged upon the anvil of God's sovereign purpose, but he has felt the heart throb and heard the soul cry of as many people as any preacher of this century. He has walked among the masses, ministering to the soul needs of people. He is truly a tool, tried in many fires of the Lord's battles and always shines the brighter after conflict for Christ.

B. R. Lakin has no peer as a preacher. He was gifted by God with a scintillating brilliant mind and masterful eloquence. He has been divinely endowed with an immeasurable amount of ability. All of this talent has been completely dedicated to the service of the Lord Jesus Christ. I have often watched him take the Word of God and go to work on an audience as a skilled surgeon goes about his task. I have listened to him preach when it seemed that a heavenly halo had settled about him. Then I have witnessed God putting His stamp of approval upon this man of God as multitudes came to be saved, and many lives have been blessed and changed.

The many faceted ministry of this man of God cannot be exaggerated. Dr. Lakin has no equal as a pulpiteer but his life outside of the pulpit has not been one of mediocrity. His influence upon preachers, his ministry and counsel to individuals is unsurpassed in excellency. He has been the preacher's friend, the church's helper, the common man's leader and most of all, he has been for fifty-two thrilling, fruitful years, God's mighty messenger. His sons in the ministry are all over America and converts are all over the world. What a God-send is his message, the voice of one of the truly great preachers of all time. As a Christian, his devotion to Christ is unquestioned. As a trusted friend, he is pure gold.

Yes, from the obscurity of the "Forks of the Big Sandy," has come this divinely-sent human meteor to pass among men and move them to Christ and His Cross. As our generation speaks of Spurgeon and Moody and Sunday, with loving admiration, if there be a following generation before the Lord's return, it will lovingly speak of my friend, B. R. Lakin.

Dr. Tom Malone,
Pastor of Emmanuel Baptist Church
Founder and President of
Midwestern Schools

This is a day of instants. Instant coffee. Instant tea. Instant dinners. Instant Greek students. Instant Hebrew students.

It's a day when foolish parents want their children to become instant adults. Little girls are taken to the hair dresser. Little boys become grown-ups.

And there are instant evangelists with their instant success. And any number of them, void of genuine convictions, experience and maturity and the perspective and stability that go with these qualities, have come to a pathetic and tragic end.

Dr. B. R. Lakin is not an instant preacher. He is not an instant evangelist. He was never an instant "success." He was a child, a boy, a young man, a middle-aged man, and now he is 72. He is the husband of a wife of more than forty years. He is the father of a dead son, his only child.

He was converted in a church at the forks of a creek in the mountains of his native West Virginia, during a revival meeting. He went to a service during that meeting to get converted. He knew what he wanted. He got what he wanted.

Following his conversion, he became a Baptist preacher. He rode a mule across the West Virginia mountains to preach the Gospel. It was the same Gospel he is preaching today, after more than fifty years.

No man on a mule in the West Virginia mountains is an instant success—not when a "high day" in his Sunday school is an attendance of 18.

Dr. Lakin stuck to his work. Having put his hand to the plow, the debate was over. He had one thing to do—preach the Gospel.

There were the great days of Cadle Tabernacle in Indianapolis. And those daily radio broadcasts over one of the most powerful radio stations on earth. And the crowds that assembled at the tabernacle. And the great and powerful preachers and evangelists who preached there, and felt honored to know the man who had invited them there.

The atmosphere was stimulating in those days. Outstanding preachers were somebody in those days. Those were not the days of instants.

But those days passed away. The tabernacle became mostly a memory.

What did Dr. Lakin do?

He didn't mystically and emotionally cling to the past—as most men under such circumstances have done. He didn't believe that the only place you could find any good was in the cemetery. He believed that there was still important work to be done.

He started preaching with a zeal, a determination, and a success he had never had before. In all kinds of churches, large and small, in prominent places where there were modern conveniences, in primitive places where there were next to none.

There is no work on this earth more strenuous than the work Dr. Lakin is doing. There is no work more spiritually, mentally, emotionally, and physically exhausting.

Yet he keeps it up year after year.

How does he keep at it?

Because he has deep convictions that God called him to preach as long as God would give him the strength.

Because he has a character that has been molded by experience; by pain and sorrow and disappointment and loneliness; by a faith that has sustained him when the stars have left the sky.

Dr. Lakin is, first of all, an honorable man. He possesses the qualities a Christian gentleman ought to possess.

He is what they used to call a pulpiteer. He is one of the most attractive and effective speakers in the country. And he always works and speaks for a verdict—sinners confessing Christ.

Noel Smith, Editor Baptist Bible Tribune, Springfield, Missouri

FOREWORD

To be commissioned to such a task as writing the Biography of a man like Dr. B. R. Lakin is a rare privilege few men will ever have. On the other hand, the responsibility is astronomical, challenging and frightening. This effort was undertaken with fear and trembling, recognizing I did not have the ability to do the book justice. Dr. Lakin is deserving of much more than this writer is capable of delivering.

The material in this book has been collected, arranged and prepared for publication with prayers and tears. Dr. Lakin has been my Christian Hero since I was a child. I was saved at the little log Methodist Church where Dr. Lakin conducted his first Revival Meeting. At the time I was converted he was pastor of the world famous Cadle Tabernacle in Indianapolis, Indiana. As a barefoot, country boy I would hurry home from the services at the old log church to hear Dr. Lakin preach over the radio. My ear was fastened to the old battery-powered radio as

I tuned the world completely out until his message was finished. I was so intrigued and fascinated by his oratorical genius, chills ran up and down my spine as my deep emotions were stirred. A lasting impression was made upon my young life.

I had no idea my loving, heavenly Father would someday permit me to share the pulpit with this giant of the faith and write his Biography. While the effort has cost hours of sleep, sacrifice of time and many days of research it has been a great joy fellowshipping with Dr. Lakin and getting to know him more intimately. I will be well rewarded for my small contribution if only Jesus Christ is exalted and His servant, Dr. Lakin is able to share God's message with more people through my feeble efforts.

It would be profitable for men and honoring to God if every young minister in America made a thorough study into the life of Dr. B. R. Lakin.

W. K. "Kenny" McComas

Mr. and Mrs. Richard Lakin—Parents of Dr. B. R. Lakin.

1

"A CHILD IS BORN"

On June 5, 1901 a new born baby cried in a farmhouse on Big Hurricane Creek in the hill country of Wayne County, West Virginia. Dr. L. H. York, M.D., the attending physician, announced to the happy parents, Mr. and Mrs. Richard Lakin, "It's a boy"! Who would have ever dared to guess on that warm, June morning in 1901 that the crying voice of the new born baby would be heard around the world? Who would have dared to even suggest that that new born babe would become the world-famous Dr. B. R. Lakin, whose voice crying for sinners to repent would cause countless thousands to come to Christ? The success story of that baby was far beyond the fondest dreams and highest aspirations of even those who were closest to and loved him most. It would have seemed to be sheer absurdity to have suggested that Bascom Lakin would walk out of the dark shadows of total obscurity into a bright world of fame; his megaphonic voice girdling the North American Continent daily through the medium of radio. Probably no one thought his great accomplishments more impossible during his youthful years than Dr. Lakin himself. He had no idea his name would become a household word throughout the United States. By reversing the telescope of time and looking backward across more than three score and ten years of history, it's easy to understand Bascom Ray Lakin was destined for greatness from his mother's womb.

When God needed a leader for the nation Israel, He chose a forgotten woman by the name of Jochebed to prepare that leader. She was in total obscurity, being held in bondage and servitude down in the land of Egypt. That mother was used of God however, to instill into the heart of a little boy by the name of Moses, a dauntless courage that changed world history. When Pharaoh had decreed that all male babies be drowned in the River Nile, the Bible is careful to point out, "She was not afraid of the King's command." Because of her fearless stand against mountainous opposition, the Bible also says, "By faith Moses, when he was born, was hid three months of his parents, because they saw he was a proper child; and they were not afraid of the King's commandment. By faith Moses, when he was come to years, refused to be called the son of Pharaoh's daughter; Choosing rather to suffer affliction with the people of God, than to enjoy the pleasures of sin for a season; Esteeming the reproach of Christ greater riches than the treasures in Egypt; for he had respect unto the recompense of the reward. By faith he forsook Egypt, not fearing the wrath of the King; for he endured, as seeing Him who is invisible. Through faith he kept the Passover, and the sprinkling of blood, lest he that destroyed the firstborn should touch them. By faith they passed through the Red Sea as by dry land; which the Egyptians assaying to do were drowned." Hebrews 11:23-29.

When God decided to build a Kingdom, He did so on the prayer of a mother. Because of Hannah's prayers and faith God gave her a manchild according to her request.

That man child of course, was none other than the majestic Samuel, one of the most noble souls the world has ever known.

When God chose a King for Israel, He went back several generations and began with one of the loveliest, purest and most spotless women that ever lived. The Holy Spirit records it like this in Ruth 4:17. "And the women her neighbours gave it a name, saying, There is a son born to Naomi; and they called his name Obed; he is the father of Jesse, the father of David." The King of Kings and the Lord of Lords will sit upon the throne of that boy who was exalted from sheepherding to a powerful potentate. David was God's man.

Humanly speaking, it was purely coincidental that Miss Mary Elizabeth Farmer wended her way through primitive hill country, over rough terrain from Tazwell County, Virginia to Wayne County, West Virginia where she met, fell in love and married Richard Lakin. When God needed a voice to ring out the Gospel, a stalwart of the faith and an example of courage in dark, dreary days of appalling apostasy, He joined Richard Lakin and Mary Farmer in Holy Matrimony to produce that man.

Dr. B. R. Lakin was a direct gift from

God to our generation as much as Samuel was to his generation in the day when the Priesthood was disappearing like the dying embers of a deserted campfire. Dr. Lakin's mother prayed for that baby boy long before his eyes saw the light of this world and long before his ears were ever sensitive to sounds of this universe. For a long while, his mother had been asking and waiting for that "little bundle from Heaven." While he yet lay beneath her ribs, before his cry ever became audible to the physical realm, that mother seemed to know God was moving in a mysterious but deliberate way, His wonders to perform.

Today, after Dr. Lakin has crossed both oceans with the Gospel and in his own words, has criss-crossed America back and forth like a country boy working a corn row, telling the story of Christ, he, himself would say with Sikes,

"I have worshipped in churches and chapels,
I have prayed in the busy streets.
I have sought my God and found Him,
Where the waves of the ocean beat.

I have knelt in the silent forest,
In the shade of some ancient tree.

But the dearest of all my altars,
Was raised at my mother's knee."

When Bascom Ray Lakin began his educational program, no one who knew him would have ventured so far in wild guessing to suggest that he would someday hold two of the highest honorary degrees in the land from great institutions of learning. When he enrolled at the one-room school on Queen's Creek, far back in the hills of West Virginia, in a long skirted dress, to learn the 3 R's under School Master Jake Dawson, this world offered him little or no hope of success or fame. Bascom Lakin experienced great hardship as a boy. He learned early in life the value of a friend and the value of a dollar. His day was one of toil from daylight until dark, farming by very primitive means. Every aspect of farming in that day involved strenuous, manual labor. In a humerous way, he often explains that he was allowed to go anywhere he so desired after his days' work was done. The only place he was able to go or had a desire to go however, was to bed.

He was working on a timber job while yet a teenager when God began to move in his life in a most unusual manner. Shortly after his conversion, he was called into the Gospel

Ministry. For more than a half century God has used him to accomplish great things as a Pastor, Evangelist and Author. A child was born. Because of that fact, in the Divine Providence and the Grace of God, multitudes have been "BORN AGAIN."

Dr. Lakin with horse and buggy. Riding with a friend, his only means of transportation during his early ministry.

Mary Elizabeth Lakin
Mother of Dr. B. R. Lakin

Dr. B. R. Lakin seated on the steps of Big Hurricane School, the second school he attended.

Dr. Lakin is shown here at the door of Little Hurricane Protestant Methodist Church. It was here in this small log structure that Dr. Lakin preached his first Revival Meeting. The marks of the broad axe by which these logs were hewn is still quite visible today. The foundation stones and steps leading up to the door were quarried out of the West Virginian hills and moved to the church site by mule teams.

It's quite obvious the old church building was built upon a firm foundation by the very fact it has weathered the storms through so many years. It's also quite obvious that Dr. Lakin's evangelistic ministry was founded upon the Solid Rock, Jesus Christ. From this crude log structure with rough-hewn stone steps, Dr. Lakin has gone to the great temples, tabernacles and auditoriums with their slate, steel and marble steps. The wonderful truth is, his message never changed.

This particular phase of Dr. Lakin's ministry has a very special meaning to the writer of this book. By the mercy and strange providence of God, this writer was converted to Christ as a fourteen year old boy while kneeling at the old fashioned Mourners Bench in the little log church. Although I attended Church and Sunday School here at that time, there was a man by the name of B. R. Lakin whose voice I heard over the little dry-cell battery radio from far away Indianapolis that God used to influence my life. God used Dr. Lakin to teach me how to grow in His grace and knowledge and eventually surrender to the call to preach the Gospel. Both the man and building in this picture have been mightily used of God. From these small quarters the Gospel has gone around the world.

2

"A PREACHER IS CALLED"

The husky, stockily-built, young man was laboriously endeavoring to do his share in perpetuating one of the prime, industrial resources of the sovereign state of West Virginia a half-century ago. He was separating the valuable virgin timber which grew so straight and tall from the velvety interior of the thick, verdant, mountainous forests to feed the hungry lumber and pulp mills which seemingly had sprung up like mushrooms along the many rivers and streams that helped to form the borders of the state. They sliced through the mountains and valleys like winding, shimmering threads of molten silver.

11

The timber-worn forest trails bore mute testimony to the many trips to and fro the mule had made in skidding logs from Wild Cat Hollow down into the valley, with the determined young woodsman urging the laboring beast to greater and greater efforts. He was ever mindful of the many obstacles and pitfalls which could and often did, crop up along the mountain trails to endanger the lives and limbs of the unwary. Suddenly, without warning, the mule halted in the middle of the road. No amount of threatening, cajolery, nor entreaty could compel him to move forward into the harness again. The lad gazed at the stubborn, steadfast mule with an angry glint in his eye. His glance traveled once again to the log to which the animal had been hitched to ascertain if possible, the reason for the mule's recalcitrant behavior. There were no protruding branches on the log to impede its progress. No frozen swivel nor anything amiss with the trace chains which his trained eye could discern that would cause the mule to balk. His expert evaluation of the situation soon convinced him that as he had first suspected, the trouble sprang from the innate, obstinate nature of the mule. While he stood, contemplating his next move to break the impasse which had developed there on the mountain trail, the animal, just as unpredictably as he had stopped, began to move forward again to the accompanying creaks and groans of the leather harness. With a sigh of relief, the youthful team driver resumed his place of command behind and to the right of the animal as the log, undulating from side to side, slowly snaked its way along the root-infested, rock-studded trail.

That evening, the country lad sat astride the old grindstone mounted on its rustic, wooden frame behind the toolshed, pumping the pedal which spun the heavy wheel with the renewed strength and vigor reserved only for those with the bloom of youth upon their bodies and the flush of health upon their cheeks. The cares and toils of the day were momentarily forgotten and thrust from his young, agile mind as he concentrated on bringing the bit of the axe upon which he had been grinding to a sharp, keen edge. He had learned very early in life that sharp tools were required to fall and trim the many varieties of trees which grew so abundantly in the West Virginia forests.

A statement of a co-laborer, Rev. Ben Cornutte, broke the deep concentration which had glued the boy's attention to the axe. As he lifted his foot from the treadle to listen, the spinning wheel lost momentum, the sparks gradually diminished in their brilliance and intensity in their flight upward and the dull rattle of steel upon stone faded into silence. While he paused his friend repeated, "Why don't you come along to church tonight, son?" "You might get saved and become a great preacher someday!" While the lad's dark eyes earnestly searched the seamed and weather-beaten countenance of the humble, country preacher; as he observed the love and compassion reflected upon the calm, benign face, his racing mind reached a lightening decision. Unless he was providentially hindered, he would attend the meeting that night at the forks of Big Hurricane Creek!

After his chores had been finished for the day and the soft shadows of the approaching evening had begun to bathe the countryside with splotches of dusk here and there, Bascom Lakin, with his hair sleeked down and with the best clothes he owned draping his strong, young, work-hardened frame, started out upon his way to honor his comittment with Preacher Cornutte. Thus began the turning of the wheel of destiny which would spin him eventually to the loftiest reaches of evangelistic fame.

As the boy hurried along the narrow country road, his eager steps kicking up little puffs of dirt, he could hear in the distance the clear, vesper chimes of the church bell as it rang out its harmonious message of "revival in progress" to the listening countryside. The silvery, melodious tones seemed to swell in volume as they came racing up and down the gullies, sweeping across the fields and valleys and reverberating against the mountainsides in their quest for an audience. The ringing bell lent an air of urgency to the feet of the hurrying boy for he did not wish to be late for the start of the services.

Upon entering the white, lap-sided church building with its plain, pine flooring and pot-bellied stove Bascom sat down in the uncomfortable, rough-sawn pews and resolved to be as inconspicuous as he possibly could. That night the scrutinizing glare of the preacher as he furiously expounded upon such things as an eternal, burning hell of fire and brimstone for unrepentant sinners and the abode of a place called Heaven as the eternal reward of the righteous seemed to be focused upon young Bascom. Before leaving home he had said to his mother, "I think I'll get saved tonight." Obviously, the Holy Spirit had already begun it's mighty work in his young heart.

The divine decree of the predeterminate council of Almighty God had chosen as the speaker of the hour that night, Rev. J. C. Simpkins to deliver the Gospel message which was destined to alter the course of thousands of lives and ultimately change the eternal destiny of countless thousands of souls. Individuals, families and communities have sailed down rivers of joy and drank from the cool waters of salvation because God called His man that night.

As Rev. Simpkins preached, the quivering lad, crouched down in the pew could feel the arrows of Holy Spirit conviction pierce his heart and soul to their innermost depths. It seemed as if the sermon had been contrived for him personally. Almost every indictment, every point seemed to hit the young lad. Rev. Simpkins was no stranger to sin and evil. He knew how and where to apply the Gospel whip. He was a nephew of the legendary "Devil Anse" Hatfield, one of the principal figures of the famous Hatfield-McCoy feud. This was a personal, blood-letting vendetta between two family factions who lived on the West Virginia-Kentucky borders during the early part of the century and which featured lifeless, grotesquely bloated corpses as a commonplace event, floating down the muddy, Big Sandy River.

The message, aided by the Holy Spirit drove home the awareness of personal sin with sledge hammer force. Young Bascom Ray Lakin, hardened by exposure to wind and rain, honed to a fine point of physical fitness by virtue of the demands made upon each straining muscle by the mode of his livelihood, walked up the long, seemingly never-ending aisle that night and kneeling at an old-fashioned altar of prayer, gave his heart to Christ.

A few days later, Bascom Lakin, saved by the grace of God at the age of eighteen years, stood expectantly on the banks of Big Hurricane Creek waiting to follow the Lord in baptism. Rev. Simpkins had already waded out into the water, sounding the depths as he went with a length of cut, willow branch. When he had been fully satisfied with the spot which had been selected to perform the Holy Ordinance of water baptism, he turned reverently to the waiting, singing crowd on shore and extended a tender, inviting hand to Bascom Ray

Lakin. The lad, with an outward glow lighting up his youthful features and mirroring the salvation joy emanating from within his bosom, stepped out into **Big Hurricane Creek**, disregarding the chilly waters to meet the waiting preacher. There, to the accompaniment of a hymn, he was "Buried in the likeness of Christ's death" and "Raised in the likeness of His glorious resurrection."

Heeding the call of God, almost immediately at the age of eighteen, B. R. Lakin began to preach. Even at that early age he began to exhibit the flambuoyant style of preaching and the unique personality which prophetically bespoke of great things to come in his ministry of the Gospel of the Lord Jesus Christ.

The first pastorate of the young, energetic and promising preacher was the Evangel Baptist Church located in the heart of a little, out-wayed settlement known as Greenbriar Creek. His only mode of transportation other than the natural means of locomotion bestowed upon man was by the uncomfortably slow and sometimes dangerous travel by mule-back. The young preacher, sensitive to his calling and vocation, knew that the Holy Bible, the accepted creed and principle which had changed his life and altered his

Dr. B. R. Lakin standing with clutched Bible at the Pulpit stand in Bethel Baptist Church. It's interesting to note there were 22 members in the first congregation he pastored. This makes an interesting comparison with the pictures of huge congregations Dr. Lakin later preached to shown elsewhere in this book.

Dr. B. R. Lakin standing at the door of Evangel Baptist Church on Greenbriar Creek far back in the Hills of West Virginia. This building was the meeting place for the first congregation Dr. Lakin pastored. From these crude stone steps God led His man up the steps into the greatest church building in the world.

destiny, also taught that "The laborer is worthy of his hire." His responsibilities as the pastor of Evangel Baptist Church remunerated him to the grand sum of seven dollars per month.

Many great men and many great spiritual works have started with a small, humble beginning. Bascom Ray Lakin proved to be no exception. As he developed in grace and knowledge, his preacher's heart and instinct cried out for even more spiritual and administrative knowledge. The result was his enrollment at the famed, fundamental Moody Bible Institute. In later years he has had conferred upon him an honorary Doctor of Divinity degree from Bob Jones University and an honorary L.L.D. degree from Kletzing College in Iowa.

Dr. B. R. Lakin, now a namesake of many a household in America and known for his ministry all over the world has preached to large congregations in the largest of churches. He has enjoyed a great ministry in schools, colleges, universities and Bible Institutes all over America. His ministry has extended to foreign lands as well.

Today, Dr. Lakin is one of the world's best known and most outstanding Gospel preachers. The richness of the glory of Almighty God has been manifested in his life of service in the ministry in countless ways. Although Dr. Lakin is getting along in years, with over a half-century of active, fruitful ministry behind him, he is one of the most sought-after Gospel preachers in America. Indeed, a rich testimony, tribute and fitting reward to those who unselfishly and unreservedly dedicate their lives to the service of the King.

"SET FOR THE DEFENSE OF THE GOSPEL."

This is to Certify, that after a satisfactory relation of his Christian experience, call to the Ministry, and views of Bible doctrine,

Bascom K. Lakin

was publicly ordained to the work of

The Gospel Ministry,

on the 28th day of May 1921, by a Council of Baptist Churches, composed of 31 messengers from 12 churches, convened at the call of the Big Hurricane Church at Hurricane

J. C. Simpkins Moderator.

L. L. Lyaan Clerk.

A. W. Damron

E. M. Crabtree J. J. Puckett

P. H. Wilson

B. B. Kees

Carrie Crabtree

No. 103 S. American Baptist Publication Society, Philadelphia, Pa.

Dr. Lakin's Certificate of Ordination to the Gospel Ministry.

(L. to R.) Rev. J. C. Simpkins. Rev. B. R. Lakin, at age 18. Rev. Vaica McKinster.

Big Hurricane Baptist Church where young Bascom Ray Lakin first professed Christ as Saviour.

3

"UNTO US A CHILD IS BORN"

INTRODUCTION

The following message by Dr. B. R. Lakin is an example of his oratorical ability. When Dr. Lakin preaches under Divine annointing, he seems to have such great command of words one would not be at all surprised if angels folded their wings, stood in silence and listened intently, stricken with awe as this master pulpiteer speaks.

Gems of wisdom flow from his lips like spray from a fountain. His message is smooth as silk and soft as butter, yet the Holy Spirit uses them to break the hardest of hearts as he drives them with sledge

hammer force. Dr. Lakin has an irresistible
tone of pathos in his voice, compassion in
his heart and such tenderness in his plea
sinners find it most difficult to reject the
Gospel. In the following message Dr. Lakin
exalts the Lord Jesus Christ and causes its
readers to envision the time Paul spoke of
when every knee shall bow and every tongue
shall confess that He is Lord to the glory
of God, the Father. "Unto Us A Child Is
Born."

Grateful acknowledgment is made by
Dr. Lakin to many people including
Lee C. Fisher for his assistance in
the preparation of this sermon.

"For unto us a Child is born, unto us a Son is
given and the Government shall be upon His shoulders, and His name shall be called Wonderful,
Counselor. The Mighty God, The Everlasting Father, The Prince of Peace. Of the Increase of His
Government and peace, there shall be no end, and
upon the Throne of David, upon His Kingdom to
order it and to establish with judgment and with
justice from henceforth even for ever. . . ." Isaiah
9:6-7.
". . . Thou shalt call His name Jesus for He shall
save His people from their sins." Matthew 1:21

As we approach THE DAY OF ALL
DAYS, CHRISTMAS, our minds, quite

naturally, turn back to the scene of THE
FIRST CHRISTMAS when Christ was born
in Bethlehem. The history of Grace began
with a Babe in an oriental manger. It's God's
way to begin small. We might have supposed
that in revealing the terror of His Majesty
and the beauty of His love, He would rend
the Heavens and cause fire to gush forth
from the bowels of a fevered world. BUT
HE DID NOT. It all began with a lowly birth
in a remote stable in far-off Bethlehem. In
my mind's eye I see the flickering torch, as
it cast it's shadow of the long-horn oxen on
the rock-hewn walls. There was no blast of
the Heavenly trumpet that heralded the
coming of the Saviour, just the muted sound
of the crunching of the cattle as they
munched their evening food and the faint,
sweet cry of a new born Babe.

The world then, like the world today, was
torrent in a maize of it's selfish pursuit.
There was no room for Jesus in the Inn.
Truly, "He came to His own and His own
received Him not." He was the descendant
of David. He was also the rightful Heir to
the City of David, in which He was born.
It was His by right of inheritance—"But
there was no room for Him in the Inn."
Even though we all belong to Him by right

of creation, blundering mankind today, after nearly two thousand years of Grace, is still crowding Jesus out of His rightful place in the hearts of men.

IT ALL BEGAN WITH A BABE IN BETHLEHEM. God ever uses the weak things to confound the mighty. Hundreds of years ago, men were following with baited breath, the march of Napoleon and waiting with feverish impatience for the latest news of the wars. Meanwhile, in the homes of the nations, God worked in a quiet, powerful way. Babies were being born, but who had time to think of babies—everyone was thinking about battles.

In that year of bloody conflict—Gladstone was born in Liverpool, Alfred Tennyson was born in the Summerfield Rectory, Oliver Wendell Holmes was born on the shores of a new world, Abraham Lincoln was born in Kentucky and Felix Mendelssohn was born in Hamburg. Men fought and killed in their alleged efforts to free the world, but God was bringing into being emancipators, poets and musicians who were to make the world a better place in which to live. We sometimes fancy that God can only manage His world by big battalions abroad but all the while, He is doing it by creating little babies who will grow up to alter the course of human progress. When a wrong needs righting or when a truth needs presented and our race needs redemption, God sends a baby into the world to do it. THAT'S WHY JESUS WAS BORN IN BETHLEHEM. "Unto us a Child is born." That speaks of God's identification with man. As John puts it,—"The Word was made flesh and dwelt among us."

The First Christmas, a White Night, was all wrapped up with beauty. The richness of the truth is in John 3:16—"For God so loved the world that He gave His only begotten Son, that whosoever believeth in Him should not perish but have everlasting life." And the angel said—"Thou shalt call His name Jesus, for He shall save His people from their sins," coupling the Prophesy of Isaiah with the name given Him by the angels.

JESUS. I want to use the letters of His name to remind us of His wonderful attributes. I would like to take that first letter "J" and say from it, I received the "JUST ONE." Isaiah said, "Of the increase of His Government and peace, there shall be no end, and to establish it with justice and judgment from henceforth even for ever" . . . In Acts 7:52, He is called "The Just

One." The world has never known a perfect man. Even David, the favorite of God, committed a selfish, cowardly, immoral sin and God severely punished him for it. Moses sinned, Sampson sinned and Saul sinned. The record of mankind is besmirched with the scarlet blemishes of transgression but Jesus is "The Just One." Who in the land is without spot or blemish? Jesus alone, is wholly righteous and wholly qualified to be the Redeemer of the race.

The centuries have proven Him to be all that He claimed to be. When He was on the earth He traveled no great distances from the obscure, little village where He was born and yet there was a great pilgrimage from the ends of the earth to see where Christ was born. He raised no armies, caused no violence and yet millions have fought for the faith He inspired. He wrote no books and yet the lands of the world are filled with books written by the noblest minds of the years about Him. He sang no songs and yet the world's greatest music has been inspired by His life. He organized no church and yet today there are millions of church spires pointing Heavenward to Him who sits at the right hand of God, interceding for us. He wrote no Philosophy and yet Philosophers of the centuries have based their theories upon His teachings. He was THE JUST ONE, who justifies all who come to Him for forgiveness of sins.

He not only preached that He was the Son of God, but His conduct proved that He was. No one, except God, could live in the muck and mire of a sinful world without being contaminated by the sin of the race. "All have sinned and come short of the Glory of God" and "All we, like sheep, have gone astray, we have turned everyone to his own way and the Lord has laid upon Him the iniquity of us all."

He was The Prince of Peace. Princes inevitably become Kings. One day he shall be King of Kings and Lord of Lords. *WITH RESPECT*, we surrender to THE JUST ONE, who shall rule His kingdom forever with justice and judgment. *WITH REVERENCE*, we look at Him, whose death was ignominious and whose Resurrection was glorious. *WITH ADMIRATION*, we behold "THE JUST ONE," whose WISDOM, POWER AND GLORY shall pass the compensation of mankind.

Fairest Lord Jesus, Ruler of all nature,
Oh, Thou of God, man and the Son;

Thee will I cherish, Thee will I honor,
Thou my soul's glory, joy and crown.

Now, may we consider the "E"? HE IS
OUR EMANCIPATOR. The word Emancipator means "Deliverer" or one who sets
free from bondage. In Christ's first sermon
in Nazareth, He said, "—I am sent to deliver
the captive from bondage." Humanity was
shackled and chained by sin. The inherent
evil from Adam and from Adam's dominage
of the race prevailed. The blight of mankind
was worse than that of a prisoner but in
one powerful, liberating act upon the cross,
Jesus snapped the chains that held mankind
and set them free: This was the drive, the
incentive, the dominating factor in His life.
"To this end was I born, for this cause came
I unto the world," He said as He set His
face toward Jerusalem and Calvary.

We, in America, are familiar with the
Emancipation Proclamation which was issued
by our Abraham Lincoln. For millions of
slaves it was a great day when it was
signed. The Proclamation was taken to Mr.
Lincoln at noon on the first day of January,
1863 by Secretary Seward. As it lay unrolled
before him, Mr. Lincoln took a pen, dipped
it in ink and moved his arm toward the

place for his signature, then held it for a moment. He then removed his hand and dropped the pen. After a little hesitation he again took up the pen and trembling said to Mr. Seward, "I have been shaking hands since 9 o'clock this morning and my arm is almost paralyzed. If my name ever goes down in history, it will be for this act and my whole soul is in it. If my hand trembles when I sign the Proclamation, all who examine the document will say, 'He hesitated'." Then he turned to the table, took up his pen and slowly but deliberately, with firm hand wrote *"Abraham Lincoln."* He looked up, smiled and said, "That will do."

JESUS, THE GREAT EMANCIPATOR. Jesus did not hesitate to effect the Emancipation Proclamation with His own blood and liberate mankind from the bondage of sin. Not just one race but the whole world.

> Guilty, vile and helpless we,
> The spotless Lamb of God was He.
> Full atonement can it be,
> Hallelujah, what a Saviour!

May we also consider the "S" and that is, THE SIN BEARER." . . . The Lord hath laid upon Him the iniquity of us all." Isaiah 53:6. I see the dim light in the stable at

Bethlehem as it flickers in the soft night air. It's rays shine across the straw-strewn manger room and strikes an upright timber and crossbar. I see the shadow of a cross on the wall by the new born infant's crib. Born to be crucified and yet He willed it so. "He who was rich became poor that we, through His poverty, might be made rich." *He literally lived under the shadow of the cross.* He was not called "A Man of Sorrow" because He was sorry about the inevitable cross but because His heart was broken by the sins that have broken mankind. He, in His earthly Ministration, was discharging His responsibility as The Lamb Of God that taketh away the sins of the world and He was accomplishing it victoriously. "Who, being the brightness of His Glory; and express image of His person and upholding all things by the Word of His Power, when He had, Himself, purged our sin and sat down on the right hand of Majesty on High."

In the Old Testament there is a beautiful type of Christ's redemptive work in the scapegoat. A clean, spotless animal was selected from the flock. "And Aaron shall lay his hands upon the head of a live goat, all the transgression of their sins being put upon his head." Christ, our Sin Bearer, became

THE LAMB OF GOD that taketh away the sin of the world. Just as the scapegoat of the Old Testament carried the iniquities of God's children into a land not inhabited, so Jesus Christ took our sin far away so that God could see and remember them no more.

Now, may we momentarily consider the "U"? I like to think of it as THE UNDER-STANDABLE FRIEND. Jesus said to His Disciples, "I call you not strangers but friends." The word "friend" is perhaps the warmest, most tender word in the English Language. What more inspiring Hymn do we sing than "What A Friend We Have in Jesus?" It never grows old because it expresses a truth and it's truth is always fresh, inspiring and alive. Before Christ was born in Bethlehem the world had never thought of God as a friend. God was a person unapproachable. Jesus was companionable and friendly with all kinds of men.

He dined with sinners.
He consorted with men of nobility.
He conversed with the dubious character at Jacob's well.
He rubbed shoulders with lepers.
He fraternized with fishermen.
He hobnobbed with the multitude.

And through Him the world was made to know that God was loving, kind, compassionate and merciful. He was not an unapproachable Majesty in the far, distant Heavens who cared nothing for mankind. "Like a father pitieth his children, so the Lord pitieth them that fear Him."

During my visit to Honolulu I rejoiced to hear the many testimonies from Chinese, Japanese, Korean and Hawaiian Christians about the fellowship they find in Christ. A Chinese Christian gave this testimony. "I had fallen into a deep, dark pit and lay in it's miry bottom, groaning and unable to move. A man passed by close enough to hear my cry but he walked on without making any effort to help me." *THAT IS MOHAM- MADISM.* Confucious walked by the edge of the pit and said, "Poor fellow, I am sorry for you. Now, let me give you a piece of advice. If you ever get out of there, don't get in again." Don't get in again—*THAT IS CONFUCIOUS.* A Buddhist Priest came by and said, "Poor soul, I am very much pained to see you there. I think if you could get out two-thirds of the way, I might be able to assist you the rest of the way." But, I was unable to help myself. *THAT'S BUDDHISM.* Then I saw THE SAVIOUR standing on the edge of the pit. He reached down with His nail-scarred hand and said, "Friend, give me your hand." He lifted me out and set my feet upon a solid rock. *THAT IS CHRISTIANITY*. Yes, He is a Friend. If the world would only learn to lift it's pale and trembling hand and take hold of His pierced hand, half the world's ills would be cured.

The last letter of alliteration is "S", SAVIOUR OF THE WORLD. "Thou shalt call His name JESUS. He shall save His people from their sins." Oh, my friend, if God can paint the blush on the bud that hangs from the lip of the rose and make the dew drops of the morning tremble like molten diamonds on the white lip of the lily. . . . If He can paint the rivers in lines of rippling silver and cover valley floors with carpets of softest green, tacked on with lovely daisies and laughing daffodils. . . . If He can scoop out the basin of the Seven Seas and pile up the great granite mountains until they pierce the turquoise sky. . . . If He can send the Niagara thundering on its mighty and majestic ministry from century to century. . . . If He can fuel and refuel the red-coated suns to blaze with universal light. . . . If on the looms of Heaven He can weave the delicate tapestry of the rainbow and at eventide fashion a fleece of crimson to curtain the couch of a dying man. . . . And across the black bosom of the night that follows, bind the quivering girdles, spangled with ten thousand studded jewels, then I, as a rational man, cannot doubt His power to save the lowest sinner and transform the snobs of Society by the miracles of the New Birth.

That night, in Judean skies, the mystic star
    dispensed it's light,
A blind man moved in sleep and dreamed
    that he had perfect sight.
That night, when shepherds heard the angel's
    song and moved about with fear,
A deaf man moved about and dreamed that
    he could clearly hear.
That night, within the cattle stall slept Child
    and mother cold,
A cripple moved his twisted limbs and
    dreamed that he was whole.
That night, with new born babe, a tender
    Mary arose to lean over a stable wall,
    when a loathsome leper smiled in sleep
And dreamed that he was clean.
That night, within the mother's breast the
    little King was held secure,

A harlot slept a happy sleep and dreamed
    that she was pure.
That night, within the manger laid The
    Sanctified who came to save,
A dead man moved in sleep of death and
    dreamed there was no grave.

That's the Jesus I've tried to present to a
lost world for more than a half century.

    For time and for Eternity
    For life and the valley between
    And the land beyond.

I wonder if you have room for Jesus today
in your heart? "Behold I stand at the door
and knock. . . ." Revelation 3:20. Let Him
in, won't you?

4

"AMERICA'S GREATEST NEED"

INTRODUCTION

There are four loud, long and lasting cries being made to the American people today. Some say, "Learn," some say, "Earn," others say, "Burn," still others say, "Turn." The group crying "Learn" claim education is needed to cure the ills of our Society. Those who insist on earning higher wages say economic development is the answer to our problems. The loudest cry of all is being chanted by the rebellious crowds who are attempting to lead the masses into political anarchy with, "Burn, baby, burn." Dr.

Lakin stands firm with a minority group crying, "Turn!."

His cry, like Moses of old, is "Repent and turn to God before we pass the point of no return." He believes God's promise is still valid. "If my people which are called by My name shall humble themselves and pray and seek My face; and turn from their wicked ways; Then will I hear from Heaven, and will forgive their sin, and will heal their land."

Dr. Lakin constantly reminds the church today that God's final word to her is, "Repent or be removed." "Except thou repent I will come and remove the candlestick out of it's place" was the last message of Christ to the church.

Dr. Lakin joins the Poet in saying—

What's happened in America?
Does some new power rule,
Whose force is felt in home and church,
And even in the school?

If I express my loyalty,
For what I hold so dear,
I'm prejudiced, a stubborn fool,
And even insincere.

If I stand up against the wrong,
As Christ would bid me stand,
I'm scoffed and ridiculed
Folks just don't understand.

And even when I talk to God
Who answers when I pray
They look at me and laugh again,
Oh, it's just luck, they say,

Yet, still with Christ, I take my stand
Against endless criticism
And fight the foe with all my might,
The power of Godless communism.

The following sermon by Dr. B. R. Lakin entitled "America's Greatest Need" has been read into the Congressional Record by the Honorable Congressman William Jennings Bryan Dorn of South Carolina on October 3, 1968. Congressman Dorn made the following introductory remarks before reading the sermon into the Record.

Mr. Dorn. "Mr. Speaker, it was my great privilege to attend the Haven of Rest Mission's eighth anniversary dinner on Saturday night, September 21, 1968, at the Holiday Inn, Anderson, South Carolina.

My warm personal friend, the Reverend

Hugh Parsons, founder and superintendent of the Haven Rescue Mission and Children's Home has the answer to poverty, disease and moral decay so evident in our country today. His mission is a classic example of what can be done and what is right and good about America. Mr. Parson's anniversary banquet was an occasion I will long remember. My friend, Rev. Robert Martin was Master of Ceremonies. Many distinguished political leaders, ministers, and members of the Mission Board were present to hear the following outstanding and timely address by Dr. B. R. Lakin of Fort Gay, West Virginia."

AMERICA'S GREATEST NEED

"The Lord liveth, in truth, in judgment, and in righteousness; and the nations shall bless themselves in Him, and in Him shall they glory." (Jeremiah 4:2.)

In these days of national strife and international confusion, when the seeds of hatred are being cultivated in the hotbeds of Communism and radicalism, let us throw back our shoulders, double up our fists (rough with the callouses of honest toil) and stand up for true, fundamental, Godly Americanism.

The Bible teaches patriotism and patriotism was the light that burned in the hearts of the faithful in the midnight gloom of the dark ages. It was the torch that lit the fires of the Reformation. It was the rock upon which Western civilization was founded. And if our civilization survives the onslaught of the Red Scourge it will be Christian patriotism that will fuel the lamps of truth and provide morale for the fight for freedom.

AMERICA HAS MANY PRIVILEGES

America has many privileges but it also has great responsibilities. Just as our freedom was obtained at a great price, our first responsibility is to God but we are duty-bound to our beloved country.

"Let every soul be subject unto the Higher Powers. For there is no power, but of God; The powers that are ordained of God."

Sir Walter Scott struck a note of true Christian Patriotism when he wrote—

"Breathes there a man with soul so dead,
Who never to himself hath said,
'This is my own, my native land?'
Whose heart hath e'er within him burned,
As home his footsteps he hath turned,
From wandering on a foreign strand?
If such there breathes, go mark him well:

For him no minstrel raptures swell,
High though his titles, proud his name,
Boundless his wealth as wish can claim,
Despite those titles, power and pelf,
The wretch, concentered all in self,
Living shall forfeit fair renown,
And double dying shall go down
To the vile dust from whence he sprung,
Unwept, unhonored and unsung."

With man-made creeds forgotten, we find common ground in the sublime truth of the "Old Book." And in the spirit of those brave men who crossed the seas in search of a free land, in which they could worship their God according to the dictates of their hearts.

We enjoy the benefits of a land founded in faith; baptized in blood and dedicated to the freedom of worship. I would like, by the help of the Spirit, to revive within our hearts some of the great ideals that have made America the "Hub", the very center upon which the world revolves. I would like to stir up our souls with a renewed national zeal and a closer walk with God, without whom no nation can succeed.

I. WE NEED A SENSE OF GRATITUDE

One day in every year we celebrate Thanks-

giving but one day in 365 days is not enough.
Americans should thank God every day that
we live in "The Land Of The Four Free-
doms." Every day we should thank God for
the sacrifice of blood, sweat, privation and
even death on the part of the multiplied
thousands of our heroic dead. Had it not
been for their standing between us and the
iron hand of Fascism and Nazism, we might
not be commemorating their sacrifice. Instead, we might be goose-stepping at the
heels of storm troopers and taking our orders from them instead of the Bible being
read in our beloved homes. "Mein Kampf"
might now be our text book. Instead of blend-
ing our free voices in the singing of "My
Country, 'Tis of Thee," we might be "Heil-
ing," and saluting the Swastika.

Let us bow our heads in humility and let
us bow our hearts in reverence and gratitude
to a merciful God, who has brought us national deliverance and for this let us be sincerely grateful.

(1) We should be grateful for the righteous birth of our native land.

Other nations were born in the blood of
plundering conquest, but not America. This
nation was conceived in the noble hearts

of courageous, righteous men. It was born in the throes of Holy Prayer at Plymouth Rock. It was cradled by the strong hand of stalwart faith and nourished at the bosom of living, vital, sincere religion. It was fed on the wholesome food of the highest ideals and developed to it's towering stature under the smiling approval of Almighty God.

America stands today, a fortress of freedom, loved by all free men; respected by the liberty-loving peoples of the earth; feared by the enemies of God and human liberty. With the shadows of Communism deepening upon every continent, America holds high the torch of faith, light and hope for the downtrodden peoples of the world.

(2) We should be grateful for our natural, industrial and scientific resources with which we have been blessed.

Because of our giving God His rightful place at the outset of our national life, God smiled and gold poured from the rocky crags of the Golden West. God smiled and wide acres of grain sprang from the soil of the Middle West. God smiled and the picturesque hills of The East yielded black gold in ample abundance to warm our hearths and turn the wheels of industry. God smiled and the

automobile, the aeroplane and a thousand
and one industrial miracles took place before
our very eyes. God smiled and has seen to
it that Old Glory has never dipped her colors
to any Atheistic, God-hating, man-enslaving
country. God smiled and our scientists
brought into being the atomic bomb, which
is destined to be that paradoxical instrument
of destruction to save men from destruction.

Today, WE STAND IN A PRECARIOUS
POSITION IN REGARD TO OUR
NATIONAL LIFE.

We, as a Nation, must do nothing to invoke
the frown of Almighty God upon us. Our
course must be such as to keep Heaven's
smile upon our beloved country. We stand
at the crossroads. To the left, lies the bogs
of extreme liberalism, socialism and the inevitable drift into Communism. To the right,
lies the time-worn swamps of ultra-conser-
vatism which leads to monopolies of certain
groups at the expense of other groups.

We must keep in the middle of the road
and prayerfully seek the guidance of God
or our nation will go the way of all other
nations in past history—in oblivion. It is the
approval of God that makes a country great,
not the genius of statesmen; not merely the

form of government; nor the energy of it's
people but the level of the National Morals
and the depth of the National Faith in God.

Not serried ranks with flags unfurled,
Not armoured ships that gird the world,
Not hoarded wealth nor busy mills,
Not cattle on a thousand hills,
Nor sages wise, nor schools nor laws
Not boasted deeds in Freedom's cause—

All these may be, and yet the state
In the eye of God be far from great,
That Land is great which knows the Lord,
Whose songs are guided by His Word;
Where justice rules, 'twixt man and man,
Where love controls in art and plan;
Where, breathing in His native air,
Each soul finds joy in praise and prayer—
Thus may our Country, good and great,
Be God's delight—man's best estate.

(3) We should be thankful for our homes.
Though many of our citizens have brought
reproach on the American home, by their
selfish and loose living, it still remains our
greatest heritage. The meaning of the word
"Home" is so foreign to some people of the
world that the equivalent of the word is not

even in their language. The American traveler abroad, when he sees the condition existing in some foreign families, comes into a new appreciation of our home life in this country.

Henry Van Dyke once wrote after a trip abroad,
"So it's home again, and home again,
America for me!
My heart is turning home again
And there I long to be;
In the land of youth and freedom,
Beyond the ocean bars,
Where the air is full of sunlight,
And the flag is full of stars."

Thank God for a part in guiding the American home in spiritual things. For years, every morning, a radio poll showed I spoke to 800,000 people over the Nations Family Prayer Period. People from all walks of life, gathered before their radios at the beginning of the new day to "Look into His face" and listen to His Word. We need a revival of interest in spiritual matters today.

II. WE NEED A GREATER CONSCI-OUSNESS OF OUR RESPONSIBILITY.
Our greatest sin as a Nation is the sin of

complacency. Smugness is the forerunner of indifference and indifference is the predecessor of national deterioration. As the old saying goes, "A chain is no stronger than it's weakest link." It can be truthfully stated that America is no stronger than it's weakest citizen. This truth puts a tremendous responsibility upon every one of us.

The forces of Anti-Americanism and Anti-Christianity are at work in our beloved land. Most of their work is sinister and undercover but like leaven, they seek to eventually leaven the whole lump of our way of life and supplant regimented, centralized totalitarianism for old fashioned, red-blooded, stalwart Americanism.

This leaven of Atheism is found in high places as well as low. No Nation ever survived a moral collapse. When Rome was in the zenith of her power and glory, sin started to eat like a canker at the heart of her national morals. Her politicians became weak, flabby and spineless. She became morally weak and spiritually depraved.

One night, while the Roman Politicians were engaged in a shameful, drunken orgy in the resort town of Pompeii, the fires of God's judgment were raging not far distant in the bowels of famous old Mt. Vesuvius, the volcanic mountain. As the night wore on, the sin and debauchery became more pronounced in Pompeii. There came a weird, sickly rumbling from the adjacent mountain. For years Vesuvius had been quiet and asleep but the hour of God's judgment had arrived. As the revelers continued their sinful indulgence, Vesuvius quivered with a mighty quake and the top of the volcano was blown completely away as a surging river of flaming, molten rock poured down the mountain in a death-dealing torrent.

There was no hope of escape. The door of God's mercy was closed for these Roman Renegades. As the lava swiftly overwhelmed the city, 25,000 people were buried beneath the flood of molten rock. This was the beginning of Rome's end as a nation. It all began when sin and lust supplanted the love for God and when gratification of the lower appetites took the place of noble character.

Egypt was once the center of world culture and their scientists were way ahead in scientific knowledge and research but Egyptian civilization floundered upon the rocks of immorality and depravity and today she is leagues behind other nations, which have striven to give God His rightful place in the national development. One has only to walk

the streets of Cairo and note the lust and the
sin on every hand, to see the reason for
her utter lack of national prosperity and in-
tegrity. A nation can rise no higher than the
average moral level of it's average individual.

EVERY AMERICAN, IN THESE DAYS
OF CONFUSION AND MORAL CRISIS,
HAS AN INDIVUAL RESPONSIBILITY
TO GOD AND HIS COUNTRY.

Not only do we have our own souls to save
but we have a great country to protect from
the fate which has overtaken civilization
just as strong as ours.

III. AND LAST, BUT NOT LEAST,
AMERICA NEEDS A HIGHER, NO-
BLER AND A MORE SINCERE FAITH
IN GOD.

"Righteousness exalteth a nation, but sin
is a reproach to any people."—(Proverbs
13:34.)

What we are, as a Nation, we owe to our
under-lying faith in God. The Pilgrims at
Plymouth Rock on their knees; Washington
at Valley Forge praying for guidance and
strength in the crisis of battle; Lincoln calling the country to national repentance in the

midst of civil conflict. These are memorable portraits of our basic faith in God as a Nation. If we have any success as a Nation we must attribute the glory, the honor and the praise to a benevolent God who has guided, with omnipotent hand, the course and destiny of our Fair Land.

In most of our wars, many of our greatest Generals were professed Christians and their decisions and strategy were mingled with sincere prayer and dependence upon Almighty God. It is significant that our enemies, as far as I know, could not boast of one Christian General in their Military Personnel.

Japan with her War Lords and Germany with her Atheistic Nazi leaders, did not have one Military Commander who sought the wisdom of God in their military endeavors. Today, as far as I know, none of our enemies are Christians.

Could any fair individual say, the prayers offered by devoted mothers and by the churches all over America, had nothing to do in bringing about victory for our Armed Forces? Suffice it to say, the enemy forces, which refused to honor God by seeking His wisdom through prayer, went down into bitter defeat and their systems vanished into

oblivion as all civilizations have which left
God out of their program.

Abraham Lincoln struck a key-note when
he said, "The important thing is not that
we have God on our side, but that we make
sure we are on His side."

Faith in God often becomes the balance of
power when two matched forces are joined
in combat, or more often, the victory often
goes to inferior forces when God's power
and blessing is upon their efforts. As Moses
said—"How should one chase a thousand,
and two put ten thousand to flight, except
their Rock had sold them and the Lord had
shut them up?" (Deuteronomy 32:30.)

When David, as a lad, dared to face the
giant Goliath, he trusted not in swords and
staves but his trust was in the Lord. He
faced the towering giant of the Philistines,
undaunted, unafraid and said, "Thou comest
to me with a sword and with a spear, and
with a shield, but I come to Thee in the name
of the Lord God of Israel, whom Thou has
defiled. This day will the Lord deliver Thee
into mine hand; and I will smite Thee, and
take thine head from Thee; and I will give
the carcasses of the host of the Philistines
this day unto the fowls of the air, and to the
wild beasts of the earth; that all the earth

may know that there is a God in Israel."
(I Samuel 17:45-46.)

We need to know as a Nation that adequate
equipment is insufficient to win a war. Germany had superior planes, tanks and men,
but they lost the last war. We must not
become smug and complacent because of our
monopoly of the atomic bomb. The atomic
bomb, without the blessing of God upon our
Nation, could never win a war.

The most potent weapon in existence is
the inward conviction that we are on God's
side and that our cause is just and right.
We not only need a greater faith in God
as a Nation, but we, as individuals, need to
know God in personal Christian experience.

Lieutenant Whitaker, speaking of his experience said, "At forty years of age, I had
never been inside a church for any reason
whatsoever, but out there on a raft in the
middle of the Pacific, I met God. I heard
Bill Cherry pray and a rain cloud that had
passed us turned around and came back over
us and drenched us with water when we
were about to die of thirst. It was there I
saw God, and learned to say, 'I believe'."
These words are from a hardened military
man who found God the hard way. Today,
he is traveling throughout the land telling

the marvelous story of how he met God. Many of us will never have the unique experience of meeting God under those unusual circumstances but we can know Him nevertheless.

We can prove His adequacy in the crucible of human experience and know that He is the Christ of every crisis. We can learn to say with Paul — "I know whom I have believed and am persuaded that He is able to keep that which I have committed unto Him against that Day".

I would rather the citizens of our beloved America should know Christ personally than for America to have the greatest military might in the world. I would rather have it said that we are a people who love God, and worship Him, than for America to have the security of the ownership of the atomic bomb. I would rather that Americans should be reverent and humble in their attitude toward Jesus, The Son of God, than to have the rest of the world acclaim us as the mightiest of the nations.

I want to close in the spirit of that touching little poem, "I MET THE MASTER."

I had walked life's way with an easy tread,

Had followed where comforts and pleasure
    led,
Until one day in a quiet place,
I met the Master face to face.

With station and rank and wealth for my
    goal,
Much thought for my body, but none for my
    soul,
I had entered to win in Life's mad race,
When I met the Master face to face.

I met Him and knew Him and blushed to see,
That His eyes full of sorrow were fixed on
    me,
And I faltered and fell at His feet that day,
While my castles melted and vanished away.

Melted and vanished and in their place,
Naught else did I see but the Master's face;
And I cried aloud, "Oh, make me meet
To follow the steps of Thy wounded feet."

My thought is now for the souls of men;
I have lost my life to find it again,
E'er since one day in a quiet place,
I met the Master face to face.

Hon. Robert C. Byrd, U.S. Senator from West Virginia and
Dr. B. R. Lakin. Photo was taken at the Nation's capitol.

United States Senate

COMMITTEE ON
RULES AND ADMINISTRATION
WASHINGTON, D.C. 20510

March 30, 1972

Rev. William K. McComas
Calvary Baptist Church
500-516 West Sunset Drive
Rittman, Ohio 44270

Dear Mr. McComas:

I have received your kind letter, and I am pleased to
note that you will be writing a biography for our
mutual friend, Dr. B. R. Lakin of Fort Gay, West Virginia.

I have great admiration and respect for Dr. Lakin, and his
life story will be an inspiration to everyone having the
privilege of reading it. I wish you success in this important endeavor.

Your prayers and your support of the position which I have
taken on the important issues coming before the Senate are
gratefully acknowledged.

With kind regards.

Sincerely yours,

Robert C. Byrd
U. S. Senator

RCB:lml

Dr. Lakin kneeling at the grave of World War Number 2 hero "Ernie Pyle." The many white crosses in the background say so much in their silent way.

DAN LIU
CHIEF OF POLICE

Everywhere Dr. Lakin has been permitted to travel in this world he has been well received. In this picture he is shown with smiling Dan Liu, Honolulu's Chief of Police.

This picture shows one of the typical crowds in Honolulu's Revival Crusade by Dr. Lakin. The people there loved him dearly as is the case wherever he preaches the Gospel. His welcome was warm when he arrived and his departure was sad as the people begged him to return again to preach Jesus to their hearts.

5

GOD'S MAN WITH GOD'S MESSAGE

"From the time I was old enough to realize anything at all, I felt that someday I would become a preacher if I was ever saved." These words, reminiscent of the man whom God had singled out to bear His message forth across the broad expanse of this great nation, spanning international boundary lines as well, had their inception in the heart and mind of a small boy while he was yet unsaved residing in the mountains of West Virginia. They were uttered by Dr. B. R. Lakin who has climbed the hills of evangelistic fame and opportunity to their utmost summit in the more than half a century of

rich, fruitful ministry God, in His gracious
providence, has allowed him.

Dr. Lakin says of his conversion to Christianity: "There wasn't any great demon-
stration, but there was a deep, settled peace
that came into my soul, a peace that stands
the crush of worlds. My mother's face shone
like an angel's that night and as I walked
out of the church building the stars looked
like they had been washed with all the purity
of God's Holiness."

Although Dr. Lakin felt from the time he
was a small boy that he was to be a preacher,
he could not have dreamed in his wildest
fancy that God had planned for him such a
ministry as he has known. This small boy,
growing up in the mountains of West Virginia, hidden away by anonymity, obscured
from the cultured masses of society, could
know nothing of the great tabernacles and
the teeming thousands that would one day
wait upon his ministry. A week after his
conversion, young Lakin preached his first
sermon and from that day until this, God's
man has been faithfully proclaiming God's
message to a lost and dying world. From the
filth-ridden ghettos of the "down-and-outer"
to the great Metropolitan and urban areas
of the upper echelon of society, the voice of

Dr. B. R. Lakin has been heard proclaiming
the Gospel. From small, humble Rescue Mis-
sions and mission churches to the great
tabernacles, cathedrals and temples, God's
man has faithfully carried the message of
hope. His message never varies, nor does the
method he employs to gain and hold the
undivided attention of his audience. He often
uses Noah's Ark as a salvation illustration.
The long-necked giraffe had to humble himself and bow his head in order to go through
the same door as the squealing pig; the
moral being that God makes no distinction
for man's honorary position regardless of his
standing in life! Dr. Lakin also exhibits the
philosophy that the preacher who spurns
the opportunity to preach in small churches
will find himself sooner or later, with no
church at all to preach in.

Dr. Lakin has been in the ministry more
than half a century. During that time he
has traveled more than a million miles,
utilizing mule back, automobile, his own airplane, and in latter years the commercial
airlines as his mode of travel. In these years
of constant traveling and preaching, Dr.
Lakin has found time to travel abroad. He
has made repeated visits to the Holy Land
and has preached in the Hawaiian Islands

and in the Bahamas. Dr. Lakin has found
time to write several books and has also
recorded fast-selling albums of his many
popular sermons. He is, without question,
one of America's greatest soul winners. It is
estimated that over one hundred thousand
souls have been saved under his ministry. He
is also a great church builder. Churches are
strengthened where he preaches. This primarily explains the reason he has always
been reluctant to engage in city-wide campaigns on a large scale. His love and devotion
to the local church ministry exceeds the
glamour and personal worship by well-mean-
ing people which surrounds many of America's famous campaign evangelists of today.

Proverbs 17:22 tells us that, "A merry
heart doeth good like a medicine." Recognizing this great concept early in his ministry, God's man with God's message was
quick to incorporate this Spiritual fact into
his personal pulpit demeanor. It has become
such a part of him that it has become his
trademark wherever he preaches. Few
preachers have made as much of well-put
sayings, odd comparisons, paradoxes, homely
applications and plain native wit as does
Dr. Lakin. Some of these laughable sayings
have been his stock in trade for years. Others,

he picks up here and there. It appears that none are ever forgotten. Those who have heard Dr. Lakin cannot forget his wit, his humor, his pathos, his burning compassion and pungent appeal. These are qualities God has given him, qualities he has used in God's service for well over a half century.

It goes without saying that a man who has attained the stature acclamation accorded to Dr. B. R. Lakin will of a necessity, have been endowed with a life of rich blessing, both temporal and spiritual, as well as one filled with zest and excitement. In the past, it has been Dr. Lakin's privilege through the bonds of the Gospel to have stood many times in the pulpit of the Akron Baptist Temple, one of the world's largest Fundamental Baptist churches, to dissertate upon spiritual things. His appearances there have always attracted large congregations which seem to become electrified with an air of expectancy before he speaks. Seldom have their expectations gone unrewarded. He has been in meetings in such places as Honolulu, Hawaii where he preached to a packed-out house. During this campaign there, he was photographed with the Honolulu Chief of Police, Dan Liu. On one occasion, the city of Richlands, Virginia turned out in full

force, replete with a brass band and a parade
to honor the preacher whom God had en-
trusted so many years before with His
precious message. Working out of Titusville,
Florida, Dr. Lakin at one time in his ministry
provided a large truck in which to cart the
"Big Top" from one location to another which
was used in his tent revivals. At still another
period in his ministry, he possessed his own
plane which was flown from time to time by
Buford Cadle, son of the late Rev. E. Howard
Cadle, founder of the Cadle Tabernacle. On
one occasion, Buford flew him to Huntington,
West Virginia to open the Tri-State Fair.
Here he was received by the Mayor, Chief
of Police, the Chamber of Commerce and a
motorcycle brigade. Indeed, God's man had
come a long way upon the road of posterity
while faithfully delivering God's message.

As a result of his widespread travels, his
many appearances throughout the nation,
Dr. Lakin's name has literally become a
household word in homes all over America.
Although he is inseparably and synonomously
identified with the Gospel wherever he goes,
he is perhaps most famous, most vividly
remembered as the colorful, flamboyant
pastor of a nationally beamed radio program
in bygone days called, "The Nations Family

Prayer Period." The program was broadcast from the Cadle Tabernacle in Indianapolis, Indiana where Dr. Lakin served as pastor for fourteen years. The spiritual, Christ-centered program was loved by one and all and is still remembered by Christians in every walk of life whose privilege it was to have tuned their radios to "The Nations Family Prayer Period."

As can be expected, no man of Dr. Lakin's persuasive ability and magnetic public appeal can long escape the ever-roving eye of the aspiring politicians. Like many successful preachers before him, he has been propositioned and assured of a seat in the Legislature if he would make himself available at the polls. Also, like the many before him, he has chosen to remain free to deliver God's message.

This amazing, beloved preacher recently spoke at the Sesquicentennial at Louisa, Kentucky where 1,000 people gathered on the courthouse lawn in the broiling, hot sun to hear him. Needless to say, he held them spellbound! When the bridge which links Louisa, Kentucky with Fort Gay, West Virginia was freed from the toll which had been instituted at its opening to pay for the construction, the event was attended by the

two state governors—Arch Moore, of West
Virginia and Louis B. Nunn, of Kentucky.
Sharing the television cameras with them
that day was Dr. B. R. Lakin. In the summer
of 1972 at Paintsville, Kentucky, Dr. Lakin
was the speaker for an area-wide campaign
in which 32 Baptist churches in the local
area combined their efforts to assure making
the meeting a success.

But perhaps the capstone of Dr. Lakin's
long, personal ministry was epitomized on
August 29, 1972 when he stood before a
congregation of six thousand saddened people
in Akron, Ohio to preach the funeral of his
long-time friend and associate, Dr. Dallas F.
Billington, late pastor of the great Akron
Baptist Temple.

Dr. Lakin was engaged in an evangelistic
meeting in Dayton, Ohio when the shocking
news of Dr. Billington's sudden demise was
relayed to him. He knew immediately that
there could be no substitute minister to
perform the funeral ceremony if it was at
all, humanly possible for he, himself, to do
it. This was in accordance with an agreement
between the two preachers, solemnized years
before, that the survivor would conduct the
services for the other. True to his committ-
ment, Dr. B. R. Lakin delivered such a soul-

stirring message and eulogy at the funeral
of his pastor friend that a world-traveled
evangelist, one of the many visiting preachers at the Akron Baptist Temple that day,
later wrote; "Oh, what a message it was!
I think every preacher there rededicated their
lives to the work of the Lord. . . . I could
wish that every preacher in America could
have heard Dr. Lakin deliver that great soul-
stirring message."

In a brief summary in the form of a letter
written by Dr. Dallas F. Billington shortly
before his death, permit me to introduce to
you the general feeling of sentiment concerning God's man with God's message, Dr. B. R.
Lakin who has remained steadfast against
the very bastions of Satan, lo, these many
years and has been a boon to thousands who
have heard him preach the Gospel. The
following article was written by Dr. Billington just prior to his home going:

"It is extremely difficult to put into a few
paragraphs the great love and admiration
which I have for Dr. B. R. Lakin. It has been
my privilege to have known Dr. Lakin for
more than forty years and in that time he
has held more than forty revivals here at the
Akron Baptist Temple.

God saved B. R. Lakin when he was around

18 years of age while he was working in the
timber regions of West Virginia. Soon after
that, God called him into His service to carry
the Gospel all over the world. His ministry
had a humble beginning. With a mule for
transportation he preached in small country
churches in the mountains and hills of West
Virginia and Kentucky. The transportation
changed as well as the size of the congregations. The automobile and jet take him
thousands of miles each year to all parts of
the United States and overseas. His strength
seems to never diminish in his labor of love
for the Lord Jesus Christ.

Dr. Lakin acquired many friends and lis-
teners while a part of the Cadle Tabernacle
at Indianapolis, Indiana. His many books of
sermons are inspirational to all who read
them. He is, in my opinion, *the greatest soul-
winner in the world today*. His life has only
one purpose and that is to preach Christ,
never missing an opportunity to glorify the
Lord.

Dr. B. R. Lakin is a pastor's friend and
he understands the problems and needs of
a pastor, having pastored in many churches
during the first years of his ministry. He is
a true man of God and no sacrifice is too

great for him if it furthers the cause of Christ."

Dr. Dallas F. Billington, Pastor
Akron Baptist Temple

Dr. Lakin is shown here speaking to a packed house at the Akron Baptist Temple, Akron, Ohio.

The following message was delivered to more than 6,000 saddened hearts at the Akron Baptist Temple on August 29, 1972. It was the fulfillment of a long standing promise to his departed friend Dr. Dallas F. Billington.

"A famous infidel once said at the funeral

of his brother, 'That we do today for the dead that which the dead had oft promised to do for us.' They had a pact between them agreeing that whichever of them should go first, the one remaining would have the service. That is the same thing that happened between Dr. Billington and myself. Some forty years ago we became acquainted when I was holding a meeting in a Baptist church in this city. (Akron, Ohio) Dr. Billington joined the church and was baptized in that meeting. From that he started and built this tremendous work that you observe today. Many, many times over the years he said, 'If I go first, you will have my funeral and if you go first, I will have yours.' I saw him not too long ago and he said that he wondered which one would go first. Well, I don't know whether fortunately or unfortunately I am left. I am left to do for him today that which he had oft promised to do for me. One by one my friends have gone. The old warriors and the old soldiers of the Cross have quietly gone away. No, he is not dead. He hasn't died. He has simply moved out for repairs, that's all. I sometimes feel like an old dead snag standing out in the middle of the field, alone. Sometimes I feel that I will be happy when that day comes and I look forward to that day with great anticipation. I have not had a truer friend on this earth than this man. He and his family have been dear to me. I have been in this church more than 50 times for special services. The last time I talked to him on the telephone he wanted me to give him a date when I could come for another meeting.

I think now of a Scripture which says, 'There was a man sent from God whose name was John.' I think that it would not be doing too much violence to it to say, there was a man sent from God whose name was Dallas. 'He was not that light, but he came to bear witness of that light.' As I read that Scripture the other night I thought of this man. It says there was a man sent and if there was anything that Dallas Billington was, *he was a man*. He was a man's man. He was a rugged man and above all, I think, he was a man of great faith, of mighty devotion, and a man of deep dedication. Besides that, I would say being a man of great faith, he dared to do the impossible. All you see here today, this great church, these buildings and the churches around the world that he has been influential in starting stand as a memorial to his Faith. All of this did not just happen. Back of all that you see, there was blood, sweat, tears, prayer and privation.

I remember in the other days when he was starting with 12 people, and about $2.40 in the treasury. Back yonder in other days he drove through the snow, sleet, rain, and darkness and not once faltered along the way. He never allowed himself to be deterred from the main issue. God blessed Him tremendously. He was a man not only of great ruggedness of character and great faith but also dedication and great devotion. He was a man, with a tremendous love for souls. For that he lived, preached, worked and toiled. When I think of him I think about that which was said about Mr. Moody. I heard Dr. Torrey say about Mr. Moody once that more than 4 million dollars passed through his hands and it did not stick as it passed through. This man had millions of dollars pass through his hands but it didn't stick. He did not use it, my friends, for his own self and for his own interests or to build his own empire. He used it for the glory of God and God blessed him. God not only blessed him with a tremendous work, but God also blessed him with a lovely family. I think much of his work must be shared with the woman that God gave to walk by his side. She is quiet, unassuming, a mother, and a wife. I am sure when the rewards are passed out that she shall receive her share.

When God looked into the future, he knew that this man would soon be passing off of the scene of action and there would need to be a leader. There had to be someone capable of carrying on. He took his own son through the schools, college, and university to equip him mentally for the job. Not only that, but his father's prayers and strict discipline equipped him morally and gave him a tremendous experience of grace and an insight into business. That was one of the attributes of Dr. Billington. He was a tremendous executive and business man.

When the time came for the torch to be passed on, there was no question as to what would happen to it. Someone has said, 'What will happen to the work when Dr. Billington is gone?' I'll tell you what will happen. It will go on gloriously because his son, Dr. Charles Billington, surrounded by faithful and true workers with a heart of concern and a compassion for souls, will be able, my friends, we pray even to reach greater heights than ever before.

I want to say that it has been my joy to know Dr. Billington. Knowing this man has

enriched my life. When Charles talked to me
the other day on the phone, I broke down.
I couldn't speak, I couldn't say anymore. He
said that he was sure that I could get someone to take the meeting where I was preaching in Dayton, Ohio while I came. I told
Him it didn't matter where I was even across
the sea that I would have come because I owe
it to my friend.

Now let me say just a word and the message will be finished. In the book of Revelation God says, 'Behold, I make all things
new.' There is something fascinating about
new things. There is something appealing
about new things. There is something interesting about seeing old things fade away and
new things come into existence. The Lord
said, 'And behold, I make all things new.'
Let me talk about new things for a moment.
I think the one new thing that He gives us
is this. If any man be in Christ, he is a new
creature. He is a new creation. He is a new
man. Dr. Billington believed in that. He did
not believe in reformation or transformation.
He believed in regeneration. He believed that
men and women born again, became new
creatures in Christ Jesus. He had been saved
before he heard me preach, but he had not
followed his Lord in Christian baptism. He

said when He heard me preach that night,
knowing that he had been saved and was a
new creature in Christ Jesus, he realized
that out of love for Jesus for saving him
he should follow Him in baptism.

If I am saved, then I am a new creation.
I am not an old something made over, but
something new from the top of my head to
the sole of my feet. I am an absolute new
creature. Before I got saved, I was just one
person. After I got saved, I became two
persons—that which is born of the flesh is
flesh and will always remain flesh. That
which is born of the spirit, is spirit. He believed that which is born of the spirit,
is spirit. He believed in that and he experienced that miracle of the New Birth.
He experienced being born again. Day after
day as he laboured and worked and toiled
and walked among men, he demonstrated the
fruits of that—that faith. Old things had
passed away.

Of course, this old body of ours is not a
fit dwelling place for that new man, that
new creation. He had this new creature in
this old tabernacle of flesh. Now we know
this earthly tabernacle will be destroyed because a tabernacle is not a permanent dwelling place. A tabernacle is just temporary.

It is just a thing that you get by in until you have an eternal dwelling (amen).—God knew this old tabernacle had pain and tiredness. That wasn't the sort of a place where God wanted this new Dallas to live in. It wasn't a proper place. So God said, 'I'll give him a new body. I'm going to put this new man in this new body. This old body is not a fit dwelling place for a new man.' Some one may say, 'What will happen then?' Well, the new man will have a new body. He doesn't have it now because this body will go back to the dust for he is not here. He has already had some big reunions up yonder. (Amen) Wouldn't you like to have seen him when he hit the shores of glory up there? Saturday night with Billy Sunday and all of those fellows. Don't you think he had a jubilee? God said he would let him stay untabernacled now. God delivered him from the old flesh, but one day God will give him a new body. When? At the resurrection.

When Jesus comes, this corruptible body, having gone back to dust, will put on incorruption. We mortal people, if we are still living when that happens, will put on immortality. (amen) Then he will have a new man in a new body. Of course, this old earth is not a good place for that. How out of place we would feel with that new man living in that new body. Yes, Dallas loved it here but he would be so out of place when he has a new body so God said, 'I'm going to give you a new Heaven and a new earth.' Isn't that great? He is going to take this new man that is in the new body and He is going to put him in a new heaven and a new earth wherein dwelleth righteousness.

This old earth is going to be made absolutely new. You look at these roses. How beautiful they are, but they have thorns on them. When you go out to pick the roses in the new earth, you won't have to wear leather gloves because there won't be any thorns. The thorns will be gone. You won't need any heart pills and all of these medications because all sickness will be gone in the new earth and the new Heaven. But you say, 'Where is the new Heaven?' It is suspended out yonder somewhere in the vast regions of space because John said he saw the Holy city, the new Jerusalem coming down from God out of Heaven prepared as a bride adorned for her husband. Won't that be great!

Dr. Billington, now the new man in a new body is living in a new Heaven with the Lord Himself. O, what glory. God promised in His

Word that we who have laboured with Him, shall also reign with Him. Lift up your head and rejoice because your redemption draweth nigh. Well, Dallas, I will have to get someone else to do it for me. (amen) If you here today are downhearted, look up! Jesus is on the throne! He will supply all your needs according to His riches in Glory.

His seat shall be empty and he shall be missed. Oh yes. But how glorious. I knew Dallas would not have it any other way. Pray for Charles Billington, his preacher son. Pray for the grandsons. Pray for Mrs. Billington. God willing, I will be coming back from time to time. I have been some places where I did not get to come back but Lord willing, I will come back here to this great church, the Akron Baptist Temple.

So I say, 'Farewell. May God bless you.' " (Permission to print the preceding message was granted by Baptist Journal of Akron, Ohio.)

Dr. Lakin and Dr. Billington Riding camels at The Pyramids in Egypt.

This writer was recently privileged to spend a few days with Dr. Lakin in his comfortable and stately home at Fort Gay, West Virginia. He rose early in the mornings and going out to the backyard fence he gave out with a hearty, "Here, Pistol! Here Pistol!" Immediately his handsome saddle horse was at the fence licking out of his hand. We then inspected the beef steers he was in the process of fattening for slaughter. We also spent a couple of days viewing the countryside, examining old churches and schools and reminiscing the past.

The optimistic attitude, jovial spirit and humorous nature of Dr. Lakin make him a most pleasant person to be around. He is probably the most versatile man I've ever known. He mixes well with all types of people. Young and old from every walk of life feel comfortable in his presence. He is truly a great man without a superior attitude. God, in His sovereign wisdom and omniscience, made no mistake when he appointed B. R. Lakin as the man to bear His message in this century.

6

HOW I KNOW JESUS IS GOD

Introduction

Dr. B. R. Lakin joins Lela Long, the great Hymn writer in saying, "Jesus Is The Sweetest Name I Know."

There have been names that I have loved to
    hear,
But never has there been a name so dear
To this heart of mine, as the Name divine
The precious, precious name of Jesus.
There is no name in earth or heav'n above,
That we should give such honor and such love,
As the blessed name, let us all acclaim,
That wondrous, glorious Name of Jesus.

And some day I shall see Him face to face,
To thank and praise Him for His wondrous
    grace,
Which He gave to me, when He made me
    free,
The blessed Son of God called Jesus.

Jesus is the sweetest name I know,
And He's just the same as His lovely name,
And that's the reason why I love Him so;
Oh, Jesus is the sweetest NAME I know.

Dr. Lakin also joins Paul, the Apostle in
saying, "Wherefore God also hath highly
exalted him, and given him a name which
is above every name; That at the name of
Jesus every knee should bow, of things in
heaven, and things in earth, and things under
the earth; And that every tongue should
confess that Jesus Christ is Lord, to the glory
of God the Father." Philippians 2:9-11

Ships of state have sailed safely over
stormy seas in times of war and strife with
men at the helm who have been influenced
by the Gospel of the lovely Lord Jesus Christ.
Rivers of civilization have cut new courses
because of the courage given to men who
have come under the influence of the Gospel

Ministry. Men like Dr. Lakin act as a gyroscope in maintaining at least a degree of moral equilibrium in a day when the world is overwhelmed in crime and debauchery. Jesus said, "All power is given to me in Heaven and in earth." We desperately need to share His power that we may be sustained in our stresses, strains and struggles.

In the following message entitled, "How I Know Jesus Is God" Dr. Lakin presents Jesus Christ as our only hope in a splendid and masterful way.

"But these are written, that ye might believe that Jesus is the Christ, the Son of God; and that, believing, ye might have life through His name." (John 20:31.)

If Jesus Christ was not the Son of God as He claimed then He is the greatest imposter of all time and the Christian faith is nothing but meaningless sham and must be discarded upon the rubbish heap of false religion.

We are facing a most important question in our subject. "How may I know that Jesus is the Son of God?" The whole weight of the Christian teaching hangs by this one thread. If it cannot stand the test of truth, then all of the alleged verities of the centuries come tumbling down. We do not hope for one minute to convince anyone by logical argument that Jesus is the Christ. We do not arrive at this conviction by mere human reasoning, but the knowledge that Jesus is the Christ must and will come by means of divine revelation.

When Jesus asked the Disciples, "Whom do men say that I, the Son of man am?" Peter gave his inspired answer. "Thou art the Christ, the Son of the living God." And Jesus immediately informed Peter that his answer was a revelation. He said that Peter was incapable of arriving at this conclusion by the process of his own reasoning, his mind was too limited to fathom such an infinite truth and so He said, "Flesh and blood hath not revealed it unto thee but My Father which is in Heaven." He said, "Peter, you did not get this merely at the seminary or college but you got it by divine revelation." Jesus said it was not a discovered truth, it was a revelation.

It is our purpose in this discussion to lead some confused souls to the threshold of revelation and prepare their hearts for the dawning of the glorious truth that Jesus Christ is verily the Son of God. If I didn't believe that, I would quit the ministry immediately out of self-respect and common decency. I believe a man who does not believe that Jesus is God and that the Bible is God's Word ought to cease preaching and sailing under false colors. I could indict and convict him before a jury of honest people for taking money under false pretenses.

Hundreds of years before Jesus came into this world, Job said he knew Jesus. "I know that my Redeemer liveth and that He shall stand at the latter day upon the earth." (Job 19:25.) Paul, who wrote several years after Jesus' ascension into Heaven, could say "I know whom I have believed and am persuaded that He is able to keep that which I have committed unto Him against that day." (II Timothy 1:12.) Even the Devil said, "I know thee who thou art, the Holy One of God." (Mark 1:24.)

If these could know Him, it would not seem unreasonable to believe that we, for whom Christ died, should be able to know Him personally, positively and intimately. The Disciples of Jesus entertained no doubt after the resurrection that Jesus was the Son of God. The writers with one harmonious voice declared Him to be God's Son, the Saviour of the world. John, in concluding His Gospel said, "This is the Disciple which testifieth

of these things and wrote these things; and
we know that his testimony is true." (John
21:24.)

We offer for your consideration several
infallible proofs of the Sonship and if you do
not know Him as Lord and Saviour, our
prayer is that through hearing these truths,
you may come to know Him as your personal
Saviour. I know Jesus, the Son of God, I
know Him personally.

First, I know He is the Son of God because
He fulfilled the prophecies concerning God's
Son. No other man born of woman could
possibly lay claim to the exact fulfillment
of Bible prophecy concerning the Son of God
as did Jesus. False christs have arisen from
time to time across the centuries but none
of them answered to the description given
of Him in the Old Testament in any detail.
The birth, life, death and resurrection of
Christ fulfilled every detail of the prophecy
of the Old Testament.

Back in Genesis, chapter 3, verse 15 is a
preview of the life of Jesus and the ministry
of Him was given cryptic though it seemed.
Yet it was an exact description of the unique
birth and unusual ministry of Christ. The
prophecy was this, "And I will put enmity
between thee and the woman, (between

Satan and the woman) and between thy seed and her seed; it shall bruise thy head and thou shalt bruise his heel." He said, "Jesus shall bruise your head. You may bruise His heel but He will get your head."

Did you know that is the reason in seminaries and colleges of liberal persuasion there are two books in the Bible they absolutely hate? These are the book of Genesis and the book of Revelation. I do not wonder that Satan hates these books. Why? Because in the book of Genesis he is condemned and in the book of Revelation he is executed. Therefore, he would seek to take these two books out of the Bible.

Notice the prophecy does not say "the seed of man" but the "seed of the woman." This is the first glimpse we have of the virgin birth of our Lord. As Jesus hung upon the cross on Golgotha, He looked at John and said, "Behold thy mother." Then looking at Mary, He said, "Woman, behold thy son." Satan at that moment was being bruised by Jesus and He, in turn, was being bruised. Isaiah said, "He was bruised for our iniquities." (Isaiah 53:5.) Jesus' death on the cross was the end of Satan's power over the souls of men. It was on the cross that He bruised Satan's head.

Isaiah also prophesied that He would be born of a virgin. "Therefore the Lord himself shall give you a sign; Behold a virgin shall conceive, and bear a son, and shall call his name Immanuel." (Isaiah 7:14.) I believe He was born of a virgin without a man in it, my friend. Some have said that was a biological impossibility. I do not think it was. I think He was born of a virgin, not of a "young woman" as the Revised Standard Version says. She could have been a young woman and not have been a virgin or she could have been a virgin and not have been a young woman but I believe HE WAS BORN OF A VIRGIN.

A person said to me, "Why, Dr. Lakin, Jesus could not have been born of a human mother without a human father." Listen, I would have you know that the first man who ever got in this world got here without either. Now crack that, you little smarty. Let me show you something. In the New Testament we read that Jesus literally fulfilled this prophecy. "Now the birth of Jesus Christ was on this wise; When as His mother Mary was espoused to Joseph, before they came together, she was found with child of the Holy Ghost." (Matthew 1:18.) There are many people who cannot accept the

miraculous fact of the supernatural birth of
our Lord. The Word says with man this is
impossible, but with God all things are
possible. You don't have any trouble with
any of the miracles of the Bible when you
place God positionally where He belongs and
that is in the beginning. Just place God in
the beginning and all the rest of it becomes
easy.

If God could make Adam without a father
or mother; if God could make Eve from the
rib of Adam and if He could create the
worlds from nothing, it would be a simple
matter for Him to create the body of Jesus
without the agency of an earthly father. You
have heard it said that Mary was the mother
of God. Mary was NOT the mother of God.
Mary merely furnished the body in which
Jesus lived for thirty-three and one half
years. She furnished the body in which He
was incarnated.

"God so loved the world, that He gave
his only begotten Son. . . ." (John 3:16.)
This verse, so often quoted by Christians,
carries a deep meaning in regard to this
truth. The word "begotten" means "to be the
father of." The word not only is defined
thus by the authors of the modern diction-
aries but it was used in that sense in the

Holy Scriptures. We may all be the sons of God by faith, but Jesus was the only begotten of the Father and in the sense that God actually begot Him in the same respect that Abraham begat Isaac. A little girl said to me one day, "Dr. Lakin, what do you do with the begats of the Bible?" I said, "I read them, what do you do with them?" She said, "I skip over them." I said, "If you skip them you will miss something."

". . . and Matthew begat Jacob and Jacob begat Joseph, the husband of Mary, of whom was born Jesus, who is called Christ." Notice that the begetting stopped with Joseph. It didn't say, "And Joseph begat Jesus." NO! Why? Because Jesus was not begotten by natural parentage and natural generation. Jesus verified this relationship to His Father in Heaven and more than fifty times in the New Testament He refers to God as "My Father." No other person who has ever lived on this earth can lay claim to such a supernatural physical heritage. It was prophesied that the Messiah or the Coming One would be the Heir to the throne of David. Listen to this: "Of the increase of his government and peace there shall be no end, upon the throne of David, and upon his kingdom, to order it, and to establish it with judgment

and with justice from henceforth even fore-
ever. The zeal of the Lord of hosts will
perform this." (Isaiah 9:7.) A man said,
"There is no Scripture that says Jesus would
ever occupy an earthly throne." I said, "Is
that so?" I told him He shall take the throne
of His father David and David never had
anything but an earthly throne. So, if He is
to take the throne of David it will have to
be an earthly throne.

The genealogy of Joseph is given in the
first chapter of Matthew. The genealogy of
Mary is recorded in the third chapter of
Luke. Joseph's lineage is only traced back
to Abraham, but Mary goes back to Adam
and Eve that we might know that He was
the "seed of the woman" which was to
bruise the head of the serpent.

Jesus could not have been the Son of
Joseph because of the curse which was pronounced upon one of his progenitors. Listen,
my friends, the man and the man of his seed
shall be properly sitting on the throne of
David and ruling in a modern Judah, but
being true seed of Joseph, he accepts the
curse of Jeconiah. Since He was born after
the marriage of Joseph and Mary, thus be-
coming Joseph's legal son, He became heir
to David's throne through Solomon. Even the

Jews did not try to contradict the fact that
He was a direct descendant of David, for
they knew the genealogical records were in
the Temple and were open to public inspec-
tion. When Jesus ascended into Heaven, the
royal lineage of David was broken, and He
is the only living heir to David's throne
with an unbroken record. The Jewish royal
genealogies were burned by the Roman in-
vaders in the Temple of Herod just seventy
years after Jesus completed His earthly
ministry. When the angel announced to Mary
that she was to be the mother of the Son
of God, he said, "He shall be great and shall
be called the Son of the Highest; and the
Lord God shall give unto him the throne of
His father, David." (Luke 1:32.) Listen,
such exact fulfillment of the prophecies cannot be passed off as we are told today. Jesus
not only fulfilled the prophecies that I have
mentioned but scores of others as well.

We may know He was the Son of God
because He correctly fulfilled all the require-
ments and all the inspired predictions concerning the Messiah, the Coming One.

Secondly, we may know Jesus was the Son
of God because of His God-likeness. In II
Corinthians, chapter 4, verse 4 it says: "In
whom the god of this world hath blinded

the minds of them which believe not, lest
the light of the glorious gospel of Christ, who
is the image of God, should shine unto them."

It is natural for a son to resemble a father.
Jesus was the very image of the Heavenly
Father. Not only are physical characteristics
inherited but traits of character are, also,
inherited. There is always a unique and
interesting parallel between father and son.
We might know that Jesus was the Son of
God because He is so much like we imagine
God to be. His conduct on earth was the
conduct of God. His understanding was the
understanding befitting to God. His wisdom,
strength and authority were God-like. He
was, as our text says, "The image of God."
Therefore, Jesus Himself, witnessed to this
truth in the 13th chapter of John when He
said, "If ye had known me, ye should have
known my Father also; and from henceforth
ye know Him, and have seen Him."

These characteristics have been attributed
to God which no other person in Heaven or
earth possessed. Omnipresence, omniscience,
and omnipotence—Jesus possessed these God-
like traits and demonstrated them in the New
Testament. You see, the omnipresence of
God reflected in the life and ministry of
Jesus when Saul was stricken on the Da-

mascus Road. Saul said, "Who art thou, Lord?" The Lord said, "I am Jesus." At the same moment Christ appeared to Ananias in Damascus and instructed him to meet Saul at the house of Judas. Ananias then said to Saul, "Brother Saul, the Lord, even Jesus, that appeared unto thee in the way as thou camest, hath sent me, that thou mightest receive thy sight." Here we see Jesus demonstrating the omnipresence of God by being in two places at the same time. He also appeared simultaneously to Peter and Cornelius at Joppa and Caesarea, once again demonstrating His omnipresence.

In Jesus' last talk with the eleven Disciples, as He commissioned them to preach the Gospel, He assured each one of them that He would be present with them, even though they be scattered to the end of the world. "Lo, I am with you alway, even unto the end of the world." (Matthew 28:20.) When Jesus lived in a physical body, He was limited in His ministry. He could not be everywhere at the same time. In His present glorified state, He is unlimited. He is omnipresent, like His Heavenly Father.

His omniscience was demonstrated on numerous occasions such as His talk with the Samaritan woman at Jacob's Well. Peter came to Jesus with the problem of taxes. There is nothing hid from the sight of the Lord. He is still the omniscient One. He knows the thoughts, the sins, the lusts and vain imaginations of each life.

His omnipotence is all powerful, like the omnipotence of God. He has power over disease. Infection, infirmities and affliction could not exist in the mighty presence of the Saviour. He is the Physician who never lost a case. He had power over the elements. The wind and waves obeyed His voice. He spoke to the howling winds and softly whining, they fell submissive and subdued at the Master's feet. He spoke to the angry waves and they ceased their fury and lapped peacefully at the sides of His boat. The devils snapped to attenton at the voice of authority and they departed at His command leaving a tranquil joy, a tranquil calm in the hearts of those they had possessed. His words were full of authority and power. Even His enemies and the Pharisees said, "Never man spake like this man." And the reason? He was not a man! He was the omniscient, omnipresent and omnipotent Son of God. He is truly the image of God.

In the third place I believe He is the Son of God because of His influence upon the world. There is no other way to account for the tremendous influence of Jesus of Nazareth upon the conduct, the epics and the history of the world but to confess that He WAS the Son of God. Born of a lowly mother, without an earthly or human father; reared in meekness in a remote town called Nazareth; without credentials from the religious leaders of His time; with no accredited education from the schools of His day; hated by the religious leaders; followed by the poor, the illiterate and the downtrodden; gathered twelve men of the lower class as His Disciples; He was called a son of the Devil because of His unorthodox birth. He was falsely accused of blasphemy by the hierarchy and mocked by the crowds which had pursued Him in the days of His prosperity. His death was demanded by the angry mob. The multitude condemned Him to die by crucifixion and He was buried in a borrowed tomb.

It would seem the world had heard the last of Him, but no, my friend, the pages of history are besmirched with the blood of those who died for Him. Wars have been fought and thrones have been abdicated because of Him. His name throughout the centuries has been above every name. His life, His teachings and His ethics have changed, altered and transformed individuals, communities, cities, nations and continents. That is the Saviour I speak about.

"I am the light of the world; he that followeth Me shall not walk in darkness, but shall have the light of life." (John 8:12.) Not only individuals, but nations have found Him the Light of Life. By following Him who is the Light of the World, the shadows of superstition, slavery and selfdom have been dispelled from the land where His light has been permitted to shine. Prostitution, political corruption and poverty have fled before His presence as naturally as night flees from day. Sin, sorrow and sensuality cannot exist in the presence of His Gospel Light.

He never wrote a book, but hundreds of thousands of volumes have been written about Him. His words have been translated into more than one thousand languages and dialects. He composed no music, yet thousands of songs have been written about and acclaimed Him as Lord. The world's greatest musicians have blended their skill in lauding Him as the Saviour of the world. He built no sanctuary but millions of churches, chapels and cathedrals have been built in

which to worship Him. He built no hospitals,
but His followers through the agency of the
Christian church have, the world over,
erected institutions of healing and of mercy
to care for the sick, the needy and the dying.
He raised no army but those who would
fight for His truth and principles the world
over, can be numbered into the millions.

The influence of Jesus has been aptly
expressed by a little poem entitled "The
Marching Christ."

"He walked the shores of Galilee,
And taught His truth sublime,
But Calvary did not stop the Christ,
He walked the shores of Time.

He marches through the corridors
Of Medieval years.
The footprints of His wounded feet
Are damp with suppliants tears.

He marches as the centuries roll,
Naught can deter His goal,
He walks the consciences of men
And heals the sin-sick soul.

He walks on through the history books
And makes His presence known,

To beggars in the market place,
To Kings upon the throne.

Though wars may come and wars may go,
This Jesus marches on,
And, "Onward Christian Soldiers" is,
His glorious battle song.

He walks the halls where nation's meet,
Where solons cry, "land-lease,"
And with His pierced hands outstretched
He offers them "His peace."

Though men may spurn His voice Divine,
As others did of yore;
He marches on, nor never slacks,
He lives forevermore.

—Lee Fisher

The influence of Jesus goes on like an eternal river through the centuries, somehow or other etching its way upon the hearts of men, leaving in its wake the transformed lives of thousands through salvation, the illumination of a lightless world.

Fourthly, I believe Jesus Christ was God because of the cross! Jesus not only lived and worked and walked like a God, but thank God, He died like a God. His life provided us with the paramount example. His death gave us complete redemption.

The cross, as related to the Son of God is one of the most significant things in the whole scope of Christian thinking. It is not a mere ornament to be worn as a piece of jewelry around the neck of a person, nor is it merely an architectural ornament to adorn the steeples of churches. Perhaps there is no particular wrong to these uses of the cross if we properly understand the meaning of the Cross of Christ. The cross itself is powerless to save but it symbolizes the finished work of Christ on the cross for the sins of the world. Because of this, it has been hallowed, respected and honored by men and nations who have come and gone through the ages. Jesus proved himself to be God by many infallible proofs. The death of Jesus on the cross was the greatest and most important act of the centuries.

The cross tells me Jesus was the Son of God. He was the manifestation of God's love. "For when we were yet without strength, in due time Christ died for the ungodly." He died for those who were unlike God and those who had been wrung out of shape and disfigured by sin. We speak of the love of God as is manifested in nature. We

see it in the glorious sunset, a ruby rose,
a vivid rainbow, or a babbling brook. But
listen to me, my friend, it is true that God's
love is manifested in the beauties of this
physical universe we live in but if you really
want to see God's love, perfectly manifested,
go to Calvary. Look with grateful heart into
the crimson pool at the foot of the cross
of Jesus and see the blood pouring from
His hands and side. See His tear-stained
cheeks swollen by the blows inflicted by the
drunken Roman soldiers. See His back
scarred and lacerated by the heartless scourg-
ing of a vulgar mob. What do *YOU* see? I,
personally, see the expression of human
cruelty, unfairness and beastlike heartless-
ness.

Look a little close and you will see more.
You will see a triumphant expression of
the love of God's Son for the world. No mere
man could die like this. This was the triumphant death of deity. He was surely the
Son of God as the Roman Centurion proclaimed Him to be.

Oh, my friends, if you want to see the
love of God you may look up at the stars and
see His glory; you may look at the ocean and
see His power; you may look at the flowers
and see His wisdom but when you look at

Calvary you will see a true uncovering of the heart of God because the cross was central in His life. Jesus was fully aware of His chief mission in the world. Little by little, He revealed to His Disciples and followers that He must die vicariously for the sins of the world. There is only one means by which man could be saved and Jesus made atonement for man's sin and reconciled man to God by His shed blood on the cross.

The skeptics ask, "How could the death of Christ, the death of one Man, exonerate man from guilt?" This is a good question and it's the very heart of the Gospel. My answer is, "If one man, Adam, could bring death to the human race, then why could not one Man, Christ, bring life everlasting? If one man could bring condemnation to the whole human race why should it seem strange that one Man, Christ could bring freedom from condemnation?"

The cross of Christ, with its upright and crossbeams, pointed upward to the Heavenly Father, the Author of the plan of salvation. It pointed outward to the far reaches of earth for lost men, beckoning them to come from every nation and plunge beneath the crimson fountain. It pointed downward to the burning Hell, my friend, and was decreeing that the sending of men to Hell should be cancelled. I know Jesus is the Son of God because of the cross of Calvary! I know He is the Son of God because of the power to change men's lives. The acid test of religion is not discovered in the test-tube of human experience. The Gospel of Christ is different than other religions of the world. As a matter of fact, the Christian faith should not be classified with other religions of the world. Let me say this to you. Simon Peter, the uncouth, vulgar fisherman felt the touch of the Son of God and was changed from worthless clay to a solid, valuable stone.

I could go on and on telling you of others who have been transformed marvelously by His power but I want to simply say this. The greatest question of this hour is not, "What shall we do about atomic energy?" or "What shall we do about world peace?" The great question today is the one that is the most vital to all people and that is, "What think ye of Christ?" Upon the correct answer to this simple question hinges your eternal destiny.

As He hung yonder upon the cross, round and round the cycle of suffering He had gone, until at last He dropped His chin upon a pulseless chest, while bloody drops filled His eyes and spattered His face and cried out between parched and swollen lips, "It is finished!" "It is finished!"

How I thank God for that, "It is finished." As the blood dropped down on His beard and ran down to the ground coagulating on the sand, the drops of blood whispered to the tiny grains of sand, "It is finished!" The grains of sand whispered to the roots of the grass, "It is finished!" Then the roots whispered to the tiny green blades of grass, "It is finished!" Then they waved their fingers to the boughs of the trees and said, "It is finished!" The branches whispered to the little birds, "It is finished!" Then the birds took off for the fleecy, floating clouds above and said, "It is finished!" They gathered it up and carried it to the gates of Heaven and resounded it down the streets of Glory, "It is finished!" Salvation is complete! Salvation is finished! Salvation is for you!

I KNOW JESUS CHRIST IS GOD'S SON because He saved me; because He offered that fountain open for sin and uncleanness saying, "Whosoever will, may come."

Dr. Lakin Baptizing Father

Dr. Lakin baptizing his son in the exact same spot he had previously baptized his father.

7

A GOOD MAN IS MOVED
BY GOD

"The steps of a good man are ordered by
the Lord; and he delighteth in his way."
Psalm 37:23.

When Paul, the Apostle, wrote his swan
song to young Timothy he said, "I have fought
a good fight, I have finished my course, I
have kept the faith: Hencefore there is laid
up for me a crown of righteousness which
the Lord, the righteous Judge, shall give me
at that day; and not to me only, but unto
all them also that love His appearing." II
Timothy 4:7-8. Paul could say, he not only
had stayed on the course God charted for
him but he had finished it with extreme

accuracy according to God's time-table. It's interesting to note, Paul encountered great opposition in his efforts to carry out the perfect will of God for his life. Even his bosom friends attempted to detour him from the course God had carefully laid down for him to follow. Their effort was not to deliberately get him out of the will of God, it was because of their lack of understanding. Note how carefully Paul explained his position. "And now, behold, I go bound in the spirit unto Jerusalem, not knowing the things that shall befall me there; Save that the Holy Ghost witnesseth in every city, saying that bonds and afflictions abide me. But none of these things move me, neither count I my life dear unto myself, so that I might finish my course with joy, and the ministry, which I have received of the Lord Jesus, to testify the gospel of the grace of God. And now, behold, I know that ye all, among whom I have gone preaching the kingdom of God, shall see my face no more. Wherefore I take you to record this day, that I am pure from the blood of all men. For I have not shunned to declare unto you all the counsel of God." Acts 20:22-27.

"And the next day we that were of Paul's company departed, and came unto Caesarea;

and we entered into the house of Phillip, the evangelist, which was one of the seven; and abode with him. And the same man had four daughters, virgins, which did prophesy. And as we tarried there many days, there came down from Judea a certain prophet, named Agabus. And when he was come unto us, he took Paul's girdle, and bound his own hands and feet, and said, Thus saith the Holy Ghost, So shall the Jews at Jerusalem bind the man that owneth this girdle, and shall deliver him into the hands of the Gentiles. And when we heard these things, both we, and they of that place, besought him not to go up to Jerusalem. Then Paul answered, What mean ye to weep and to break mine heart? for I am ready not to be bound only, but also to die at Jerusalem for the name of the Lord Jesus. And when he would not be persuaded, we ceased, saying, The will of the Lord be done." Acts 21:8-14.

In spite of all the opposition from both enemies and friends, Paul could say, "The will of God be done." By the providential direction of God, Paul could look back at the course of his life, with its many strange twists and turns and say, "I stayed on course all the way to the goal line." It meant more to him than his life.

Dr. B. R. Lakin is a man of steel stamina, dauntless courage and fearless fortitude. Through the years, he has felt that compelling, inward drive of the Holy Spirit to press on toward the mark of his high calling though it meant facing dangers, toils and strife. Many has been the time he has set out on a certain mission for his Lord when his loved ones prayed he would return safely but seriously doubted that he ever would. It would be an interesting and profitable experience for young preachers in particular, to carefully study the footsteps of a Godly man like Dr. B. R. Lakin. His course, like Pauls, also has been filled with many obstacles. Only God could have kept him from losing his way on the pathway of life.

The Holy Spirit of God, like the cross beams of a mighty radar has been focused upon the life of Dr. Lakin guaranteeing his safety and protecting his life even to this good hour.

There have been various times and occasions when it seemed beyond the slightest doubt that the ministry of this great preacher had been finished—except for the marvelous intervention of Almighty God, Who had fore-ordained before the foundations of the world that he should be divinely delivered from the pitfalls of life which lie in wait to ensnare and destroy lesser men.

There was, for instance, a particular occasion early in his ministry when he had been rushed to a hospital in Ashland, Kentucky, suffering from an acute and undiagnosed illness which to all intents and purposes, had nipped his brilliant, promising, preaching career in the bud.

The air of the hospital emergency room was literally charged with tension and stark drama as he was wheeled with desperate haste down the tunnel-like, basement hall, past the waiting patients and visitors, and on into the brightly lighted emergency treatment center, the gray pallor of death already stealing its way across the features of the still, lifeless face. Three doctors, dressed in clinically sterile, white uniforms, with surgical masks already in place, rushed to the side of the moribund figure on the stretcher to render whatever assistance they deemed necessary in order to sustain life.

The scuffling of white, rubber-soled shoes upon the cold, marble-tiled floors, the subdued conversation of the nurses and assistants; the many other sounds of activity associated with a busy, thriving, inter-urban hospital seemed to recede into an echoless chamber, to

remain suspended in silent animation, while
the doctors stepped forward with an alacrity
born of desperation and professional concern
to examine the patient. One doctor, his expression mirroring the gravity of the situation, feverishly inserted the flexible rubber
tubing of a stethescope into his ears, in the
meanwhile, his trained right hand placing
the small, cold, metal disc at various spots
upon the rigid, unmoving chest. He listened
intently for a heart beat. With his brow
furrowed in concentration, he turned to his
colleagues.

"It's no use," he stated in a calm, professional voice, "This man is dead!" Each doctor
in turn, listening and probing for the non-
existent heart beat, rendered the same professional decision. Seemingly, old Satan had
enjoyed the last laugh as far as the ministry
of B. R. Lakin was concerned because the
next day, the local newspaper went so far
as to carry the obituary of the promising
young preacher, fresh out of the hills of
West Virginia.

However, it was not meant to be! The
trained medical team, although well-versed
in the science of medicine and healing and
intimately acquainted with the crises which
often spelled the difference between life and

death for the patients involved, had reckoned in this case without the Providence of Almighty God upon the life of B. R. Lakin.

The tiny spark of life which had at first eluded detection by the diligent and trained probing of the doctors and which the devil and his henchmen had failed to extinguish in the breast of God's man, had been fanned back to a glowing flame of life, robust health and undiminished stamina. At this writing, Dr. B. R. Lakin is still living proof of the invincible grace, mercy and watch-care accorded those who walk in the Shadow of the Almighty. . . .

No man takes a hard stand against the organized forces of sin as he has done without bloody battles with the demons of this dark world. Legions of demons have camped about him as they awaited their opportunity to trip him up and destroy his great influence for God. After more than fifty years of spiritual conflict with the enemy, Dr. Lakin can say with David, "I thank God for saving my life from sin, my eyes from tears and my feet from falling."

From the Evangel Baptist Church, with twenty-two in Sunday School he was led to pastor one of the largest churches in the world. Between Greenbriar Creek and Indianapolis, Dr. Lakin traveled through many dangerous cross-roads, curves, narrow passes and dark valleys. His second pastorate was at the Ceredo Baptist Church at Ceredo, West Virginia. (A suburb of Huntington). From there, he moved to a pastorate at Louisa, Kentucky, the First Baptist Church, a church that is still carrying on a great ministry today. He later pastored the Irene Cole Memorial Baptist Church of Preston-burg, Kentucky. There were intervening periods of evangelistic work between these pastorates.

In 1937 he became pastor of the Euclid Avenue Baptist Church in Bristol, Virginia. On the first Sunday he was pastor, there were 101 in Sunday School attendance with 17 attending the evening service. In nineteen short months, under the leadership of this great man, they were consistently averaging over 700 in Sunday School and Dr. Lakin was preaching to an overflow crowd on Sunday evenings. The fresh, wholesome spirit and attitude of this young preacher was like a powerful magnet drawing people in to hear his message.

Dr. Lakin is one of the most versatile speakers the world has ever known. He holds an audience in his hands as if they were puppets on a string. When he is humorous, everyone is forced to laugh, even the stern, reserve natured people. When he is serious and using one of his many hair-raising illustrations from life, even the most proud, self-controlled people are forced to cry. Top critics say he could have exceeded the worlds best humorists and entertainers had he chosen that course in life. His wit is unequaled and at no time, under any circumstances, does he find himself searching for an answer to those who attempt to trip him up. On one occasion he was asked, "Where did Cain get his wife?" Dr. Lakin's quick reply was, "From his mother-in-law the same place I got mine." On another occasion someone suggested to Dr. Lakin that his image would be ruined for driving a new car. He quickly answered, "My family doctor drives a Cadillac and it didn't ruin him." After getting the attention of his audience with humor he makes a beeline for the cross. He exalts the Christ of the cross until hardened sinners cry out for forgiveness of sin. Dr. Lakin places great emphasis on the fact, "Without the shedding of blood, there is no remission of sin."

It has been this writer's privilege to preach many times in the Bristol, Virginia, Tennessee area where Dr. Lakin pastored. I have been told repeatedly by many good pastors how Dr. Lakin left an imprint of evangelism and soul winning that greatly affects the area yet today. Rev. Willard B. Tallman, pastor of the Tennessee Avenue Baptist Church, Bristol, Tennessee feels that God brought Dr. Lakin to Bristol for the express purpose of bringing a Revival of Fundamentalism and Evangelism. Rev. Howard Robinson, pastor of the Emmanuel Baptist Church in Bristol, Tennessee advises me he finds the influence of Dr. Lakin still prevalent in the lives of the people. This is constantly re-affirmed as he talks with people on daily visitation. Brother Robinson adds, that in his opinion, Dr. Lakin's influence on the Tri-city area will remain until Jesus comes.

Rev. William W. Pennell, pastor of the Temple Baptist Church, Kingsport, Tennessee believes Dr. Lakin kept that section of the country truly a part of the Bible Belt while other areas were turning to Liberalism and Modernism. He adds, "Dr. Lakin is the man God used to introduce the premillennial doctrine of the return of Christ to that section of the country." Evangelist Richard Ratliff follows Dr. Lakin into many churches for meetings. He says, "It's not only amazing

how Dr. Lakin's influence from the past
lives on but most amazing is his powerful
influence on countless thousands of lives
today as he preaches with the enthusiasm of
a youngster."

Rev. Gene Lasley who pastors one of the
most progressive churches in East Tennessee
says, "Dr. Lakin has made as great a contribution to the cause of Christ in that area
as any man living today." The church Rev.
Lasley pastors faithfully supports Dr. Lakin's
radio ministry known as "The Voice Of The
Appalachian."

Dr. B. R. Lakin and his co-workers arriving at Kenova, West
Virginia for a Revival at Kenova's First Baptist Church. Dr.
Lakin is being greeted by the pastor. Dr. Lakin was one of
the first preachers in America to travel in his own private
airplane.

In 1939 Dr. Lakin became Associate Pastor of the great Cadle Tabernacle, Indianapolis, Indiana. He served in that capacity until Dr. Cadle went home to be with the Lord in 1942. He immediately assumed full pastorate responsibilities upon the home-going of Dr. Cadle.

Dr. Lakin was the speaker for the widely known "Nation's Family Prayer Period" which originated from the Cadle Tabernacle and was broadcast by remote control over radio station WLW, Cincinnati, Ohio, the Crosley Broadcasting Corporation. Originally, the station operated on 150 thousand kilowatts of power. It was later reduced to 50 thousand kilowatts by a ruling of the Federal Communications Corporation. After the reduction of transmitting power, Dr. Lakin's message was carried weekly over the Mutual Broadcasting Corporation network.

For several years now, he has been in fulltime Evangelistic work. It is believed by many outstanding preachers in the world today that Dr. Lakin is the greatest preacher of the Twentieth Century. Now, after more than fifty years of faithfully proclaiming the Gospel of the Lord Jesus Christ, he is able to accept only a small portion of the many invitations he receives almost daily.

The steps of a good man have been carefully directed by the Lord for more than a half century of plowing, planting and watering. Only God knows how great the harvest will be when the season has ended.

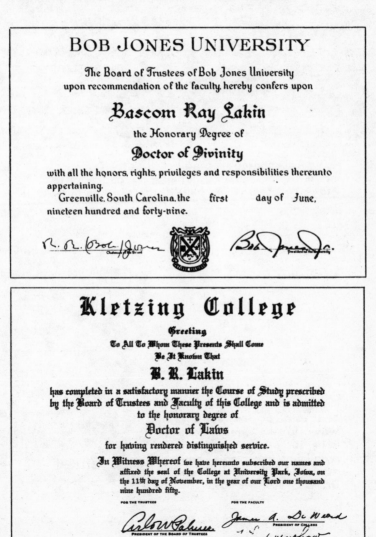

BOB JONES UNIVERSITY

The Board of Trustees of Bob Jones University upon recommendation of the faculty, hereby confers upon

Bascom Ray Lakin

the Honorary Degree of

Doctor of Divinity

with all the honors, rights, privileges and responsibilities thereunto appertaining.

Greenville, South Carolina, the first day of June, nineteen hundred and forty-nine.

Kletzing College

Greeting

To All To Whom These Presents Shall Come
Be It Known That

B. R. Lakin

has completed in a satisfactory manner the Course of Study prescribed by the Board of Trustees and Faculty of this College and is admitted to the honorary degree of

Doctor of Laws

for having rendered distinguished service.

In Witness Whereof we have hereunto subscribed our names and affixed the seal of the College at University Park, Iowa, on the 11th day of November, in the year of our Lord one thousand nine hundred fifty.

FOR THE TRUSTEES   FOR THE FACULTY

PRESIDENT OF THE BOARD OF TRUSTEES   PRESIDENT OF COLLEGE

DEAN OF COLLEGE

A typical congregation gathered at the famous Cadle Tabernacle in Indianapolis, Indiana to hear Dr. Lakin preach. Many people traveled long distances to be in these services.

Dr. and Mrs. Lakin standing near one of the entrance ways to the great Cadle Tabernacle. It's interesting to note that the years have made virtually no change in Dr. Lakin's appearance.

Dr. Lakin with brief case in hand standing in front of the Cadle Tabernacle ready to make his departure on one of his many travels. From that day until the present, demands have been so great Dr. Lakin can only accept a small portion of his speaking invitations.

Dr. Lakin arriving at Huntington, West Virginia to open the Tri-State Fair. He was received by the Mayor of Huntington, The Chief of Police and the Chamber of Commrce. He was escorted from the airport to the fair by a motorcycle brigade.

(L. to R.) Dr. E. Howard Cadle, founder and original pastor of Cadle Tabernacle. Mr. Russell Ford, choir director. Dr. B. R. Lakin, associate pastor of Cadle Tabernacle. Kurt Davis, organist. These men made a great impact upon the world through their service to God.

8

THE MEANING OF THE CROSS

The cross upon which Jesus died means different things to different people. Gross misunderstanding has prevailed down through the ages relative to Christ and the cross. Dr. Lakin takes the Word of God and marches forward in seven league boots, pushing back the frontiers of ignorance relative to the cross of Christ.

Anyone who will read the following message with an open mind, "THE MEANING OF THE CROSS" will never again be able to say, "I just don't understand what the cross is all about." This message is scholarly and profound yet pointed and simple. It will certainly speak to your heart as well as enlighten your mind.

The meaning of the Cross of Jesus has often been lost in the meaningless limbo of man's misinterpretation. The cross, as related to the Son of God, is one of the most significant matters ever considered by saints or sinners.

The cross is not a mere ornament to be worn as a piece of jewelry around the neck of a woman or something to be worn on the lapels of men's coats. Nor is it an architectural ornament to adorn the steeples of cathedrals and churches. Perhaps there is no particular wrong in these uses of the cross, if we properly understand the deeper meaning of the cross of Christ. The Communists have the "Hammer and Sickle" which has come to mean blood, force and dictatorship. The Nazis had their "Swastika," the German cross which symbolized terrorism, deceit and bigotism. In America we have our beloved "Old Glory" which to us means loyalty, purity and sacrifice. But the emblem of Christianity is "A Roman Cross" and appropriately enough, for it was on a Roman cross our Lord wrought salvation for all men, of all times, in all degrees of sin and depravity.

The Cross of Jesus has been hallowed, respected and honored across the centuries as the emblem of suffering and shame.

I. The Cross of Jesus reveals the measure of man's sin.

"That we may be able to comprehend with all saints what is the length and depth and height—and to know the love of Christ which passeth knowledge." (Ephesians 3:18-19).

A sinless God is more sensitive to sin than sinful man could ever be. We are often appalled and shocked at the depth of sin to which man has fallen. Our hearts bleed when we witness the effects of sin manifested in broken hearts, broken lives and broken homes. The reaches of the Cross of Christ present to the world the depth, the length and the height of man's sin, dramatically and effectually. It is the extremity of God's love as opposed to the extremity of man's guilt and sin.

SIN, the blight of the universe, the scourge of hell and the leprosy of the race had to be dealt with severely. Just as radium, an expensive and rare mineral, is often administered in the treatment of cancer, the cross of Christ became an expensive and costly panacea for the sin of man. Nothing in Heaven or earth reflects the depth and measure of man's sin as does the cross of Christ.

UPWARD. THE CROSS OF JESUS POINTED UPWARD to the God who devised the plan of salvation and was willing to offer His only Son, "The Lamb." who would take away the sins of the world.

OUTWARD. THE CROSS POINTED OUTWARD to the far reaches of every corner of the earth where sinful man was found. It beckoned them to come from the North, South, East and West and plunge into the crimson flood "Opened in the house of David for sin and uncleanness."

DOWNWARD. THE CROSS POINTED DOWNWARD to a burning hell prepared for the Godless. "The jaws of death and hell are broken, and the sentence of men to hell is cancelled by the obedient act of the Son of God upon the cross." Yes, it was the measure of man's sin but it not only measured man's sin, it was the manifestation of God's love.

II. The Cross of Christ reveals the manifestation of God's love.

"For when we were without strength, in due time, Christ died for the ungodly."

(Romans 5:6). We speak of the love of God as manifested in nature; a sunset, a red rose, a rainbow or a babbling brook but if you really want to see God's love manifested, go to Calvary. Look with grateful heart into the limpid, crimson pool at the foot of the cross of Jesus. Look up into the lacerated face of the Son of God. See the blood, pure and guiltless, pouring from His hands and His side. See His tear-stained cheeks, swollen by blows inflicted by the Roman soldiers. See His back, scarred by the scourgings of the mob. What do you see? Human cruelty, you say. No! That is the expected thing. That is man-like for man is depraved and sinful. The miracle is not that man would do it, but that God would permit it. Here is the greatest, the most inexplicable miracle of the Dispensations, that God would permit the Prince of Heaven to be thus treated by sinful, vile, worthless man. Only one thing prompted God to do this. IT WAS HIS LOVE. It is all summed up in one wonderful phrase— "For God sent not His Son into the world to condemn the world; but that the world through Him might be saved." (John 3:17).

III. The Cross of Christ was the means of salvation.

"And as Moses lifted up the serpent in the

wilderness, even so must the Son of Man be lifted up; that whosoever believeth in Him should not perish but have eternal life." (John 3:14, 15). There was only one means by which man could be saved. It was the substitutionary death of Christ on the cross. Through this vicarious, judiciary act, Jesus made atonement for man's sin and reconciled him to God. Reformation, education and moralization are ineffective substitutes for the atonement of Jesus. Nothing man-made could save. It was the sin of man that caused him to be lost. Nothing manufactured by him, religion, morals or learning could reconcile him to his Creator.

Creation was a Divine Act and "Re-creation" must of necessity have been a Divine Act. In that classic verse, John 3:16, it starts out "For God." In the record of creation in Genesis, chapter one, it says, "In the beginning, God." The plan of redemption or re-creation began with God. It was an act of Grace on the part of our Heavenly Father. Any religious teaching which does not recognize the necessity of the shed blood of Christ on the cross for the sins of man, is anti-God and anti-Christ and will lead it's constituents to hell, just as surely as if they followed no religion at all. We need, always, to distinguish between religions and true redemption. There are many religions, but only one that is capable of redeeming fallen, man from his sin. Those who do not embrace the truth of God's Redeeming Grace are destined to be lost forever regardless of their high ideals and good intentions.

IV. The Cross of Christ was the mark of separation.

"But God forbid that I should glory save in the cross of our Lord Jesus Christ, by whom the world is crucified unto me and I unto the world." (Galatians 6:14). All who have come to God through faith in the shed blood of Jesus on the cross are members of the body of Christ, regardless of sect, race or color. It was for that group of people that Jesus gave His life. "Christ also loved the church and gave Himself for it." (Ephesians 5:25).

The word "Church" in the Greek text is "Ecclesia" and means SEPARATED ONES. Satan hates the blood of Christ and all those who have faith in its efficacy. His spirit, in the heart of unregenerate mankind, causes men to hate the message of the blood and the cross. As Paul said, "By whom the world is crucified unto me, and I unto the world." Paul was very popular until he embraced the message of the cross of Christ. The world accepts religion, any religion, as honorable and decent. "Every man should have some kind of religion" we often hear people say but when Paul gave up his religion and embraced Christianity, he became very unpopular. The natural enmity in the hearts of his friends against the cross and its message was focused on him and he became a target of bitter persecution.

We might as well make up our minds that "The World" will hate us when we take up our cross to follow Jesus. When Jesus prayed for His Disciples in the seventeenth chapter of John, He expressed this truth when He said, "The world hath hated them, because they are not of the world, even as I am not of the world." When we accept Christ as our personal Saviour, we take on a sort of "Other-worldliness" and the world of sin recognizes us as Aliens with our citizenship in Heaven and our allegiance to another country.

V. The Cross of Christ is the motive to service.

"That He died for all, that they which live should not henceforth live unto themselves but unto Him that died for them and rose again." (II Corinthians 5:15). The born-

again believer works ambitiously for his
Lord and Saviour, *but he does not work to
be saved. He works because he is saved.* He
does not work to obtain favor with God. He
works because God has shown His favor in
the death of His Son on the cross. All
religions of the world, apart from Christianity, are based on a work of righteousness.
The Hindu hurls his body upon the ground
to appease the wrath of an imagined, angry
god. In the Orient, the bodies of little children
are often thrown into the burning craters of
volcanoes to ward off the evil spirits and to
obtain favor with their god. One may see the
"Holy Men" of India reclining upon beds of
sharp spikes, hoping to obtain a blessing
from their god by their intense pain and
suffering. All of these acts are an outgrowth
of a distorted conception of God. It is not
our suffering that counts, it was the suffering of Jesus on Calvary that completely
satisfied the justice of God. It is not our
works, it was His work on Calvary that
obtained for us the pardon for our sins. It
is not our accomplishments, it was the work
He accomplished when He cried, "It is
finished."

It is the completed work of Jesus on the
cross that compels us to serve Him. This is

our high motive for service. It is a loving
service, a grateful service and a living
service. Out of the gratitude of our hearts,
"WE *LIVE* FOR HIM WHO *DIED* FOR
US."

VI. The Cross of Christ is the melody of
Heaven.

"And they sang a new song, saying, Thou
art worthy to take the book, and to open
the seal thereof; for thou wast slain, and hast
redeemed us to God by thy blood, out of every
kindred and tongue and people and nation."
(Revelation 5:9). Heaven will be a place of
rejoicing throughout the endless ages. In
Revelation 8:1, we read "There was silence
in Heaven for only one half hour" and that
was probably when the Son of God hung
upon the cross in those last dying moments.
The angels in Heaven were gathered around
the balconies of Glory in breathless silence
as Jesus carried out the triumphant Mission
of Redemption.

We read very little in the Scriptures about
angels singing and in this final chorus,
which will resound through the battlements
of The Holy City, the angels cannot take
part. It is the song of redeemed men from
every quarter of the earth. The angels knew
no sin so therefore, could not be redeemed.

When this Song of Triumph echoes in Glory,
the angels will listen in silent awe.

Holy, Holy, Holy, is what the angels sing;
And I expect to help them make the courts
    of Heaven ring.
But when we sing Redemption's Story,
They will fold their wings and focus their
    attention upon redeemed humanity,
For angels never felt the joy that our
    salvation brings."

On a hill far away stood an old rugged cross,
The emblem of suffring and shame.
And I love that old cross where the dearest
    and best,
For a world of lost sinners was slain.

In the old rugged cross, stained with blood
    so divine,
A wondrous beauty I see;
For 'twas on that old cross Jesus suffered
    and died,
To pardon and sanctify me.

So I'll cherish the old rugged cross,
'Til my trophies at last I lay down;
I will cling to the old rugged cross,
And exchange it someday for a crown.

This tent reveals one of Dr. Lakin's many faceted minis-
tries. Whether in a tent, temple or tabernacle Dr. Lakin
always drew great crowds. This picture was taken during
a Revival in Richlands, Virginia.

Dr. Lakin is shown here by his truck used to transport the Gospel Big Top from one location to another. His home was in Titusville, Florida at that time as is indicated on the door of the truck.

When Dr. Lakin went to Appalachia, Virginia he received a royal welcome. The whole town turned out to greet him including the High School Marching Band. As might well be expected, the Revival Campaign was a tremendous success.

9

"A FAITH IS TRIED"

Dr. and Mrs. Lakin were now making their home in Titusville, Florida, the small, island-like city which had leaped into prominence overnight, partly because of its proximity to what was known then as Cape Canaveral, and which later became Cape Kennedy, and partly because of its desirability and appeal to those who were seeking for a peaceful retreat in which to spend their leisure time after the busy pace of their lives had slackened due to retirement or other circumstances.

Mrs. Lakin, who headed a flourishing real estate business was the first lady licensed real estate broker in the area. Primarily, because of her sharp business acumen and forthright dealing with the public, she subsequently became one of the most successful.

Their own home was situated in such an advantageous location that Dr. Lakin, his family and visitors could stand on their back porch and watch the great space vehicles down on the Cape lift off their launching pads, and with exhausts streaming great geysers of flame, smoke and vapor rocket out across the Florida sky on their way to a rendezvous with some unseen, intended destination in the trackless regions of outer space. The local climate, as so many thousands of others had found, was pleasant and conducive to their health and well-being and here in Titusville as elsewhere, Dr. Lakin had an almost unlimited opportunity to reach forth across the nation via radio, the pulpit and the printed page to continue to present the Gospel of Jesus Christ to a lost and dying world.

Dr. and Mrs. Lakin's son, Bill, who was in his early thirties and in the prime of life also made his home in Titusville. Since the day of his birth on November 12, 1923, he had been a constant source of parental pride and joy to the preacher and his busy wife.

Later on in life, their joy knew no bounds when Bill presented them with their only Grandson, Ronnie. Bill, himself, was a prominent and upcoming young businessman, dealing in real estate. The Real Estate Business was booming in Florida, the monetary returns were gratifying to those who had chosen this particular field in which to earn their livelihood and economically speaking, conditions had never been more promising for the Lakin family. As an added blessing and incentive to their already rich and full lives, Dr. Lakin was also at the height, the very pinnacle of evangelistic popularity and fame, preaching to great crowds at will all over the country.

Dr. Lakin was in the midst of Revival at the Chapel on Fir Hill in Akron, Ohio where the late Dr. Carl Burnham was pastor. Pastor Burnham had been greatly influenced by Dr. Lakin and they were closest of friends since he was first saved under Dr. Lakin's ministry. It was March 27, 1955. The battering winds outside the great church still howled in fury as they tore at the late-comers with a chilly, wintry edge with just the barest hint of approaching spring in the air. Suddenly, a shocking message came from Titusville, Florida informing Dr. Lakin that his only son, his beloved son, Bill had been killed in an automobile accident.

Preacher friends and concerned people alike everywhere responded in unison as they heard the sad news. "Dr. Lakin, what can we do to help?" was the anxious query upon every lip.

In the meantime, arrangements had been made for Bill's body to be shipped back to his beloved, native West Virginia for burial. Under these trying, heart-breaking circumstances, Dr. Lakin was to meet his wife there. A number of people volunteered to accompany him on the trip from Akron to Fort Gay, West Virginia or drive him there themselves, but he insisted on being alone in the reverie of his thoughts, his emotions, and grief as his mind again and again reverted to the sudden separation forced upon him and his beloved son by the advent of that prime separator and enemy of all mankind —death!

As the bereaved preacher's headlamps beamed out over the south-bound highway; as they sought out and highlighted the myriads of tiny, sparkling reflectors posted along the lonely roads, shining with the magnified brilliance of silver-laced dewdrops to warn the unwary traveler of hidden dangers, the incessant, monotonous humming of the engine, the high-pitched whine of the tires upon the pavement seemed to sing a sad eulogy. This eulogy seemed to bring into sharp, critical focus and perspective the aspiring hopes and vibrant personality of a young, fruitful life that had suddenly and tragically come to an untimely end in a heap of twisted steel, broken glass and rubble.

After the funeral and interment in the family cemetery at the top of a hill overlooking the quiet, peaceful valley below, Mrs. Lakin turned to her husband with the misty evidence of her deep hurt and grief still glistening in her eyes and mirrored in the lines of her face. In broken tones she asked, "How can we go on?" Tenderly placing an arm about his grieving wife to lend whatever strength and comfort he could at such a trying time, the great preacher replied, "Honey, I've been preaching the Gospel for thirty-five years to broken hearts across this country. I've always told them that God's grace was sufficient. If it isn't sufficient for you and me now, I've not been honest in preaching to others."

At this period in Dr. Lakin's life, God did something which was akin to what He

had done to old Abraham when Abraham
was called upon to place his only son, Isaac
upon the altar of sacrifice. Preacher
acquaintances of Dr. Lakin's all over the
land were observing and remarking, "Have
you noticed the great change that has come
over the preacher?" Indeed, he was preaching now with greater fervor, greater compassion, greater concern than ever before. He
preached on Heaven with such unction, such
fervency and clarity that his audience would
be so enraptured in mind and spirit that they
actually seemed to sit in the suburbs of
Heaven. They seemed to experience what
Paul suggested to the Ephesians, sitting together in Heavenly places with Christ Jesus.

Dr. H. Frank Collins of Bellflower, California describes in flowing terms the fashion
in which Dr. Lakin's messages are received.

DR. H. FRANK COLLINS
PASTOR
REV. JON LARSON

DUANE SHEETS
MINISTER OF MUSIC

Calvary Baptist Church

14722 CLARK AVENUE
BELLFLOWER, CALIFORNIA

August 10, 1972

Rev. William K. Mc Comas
Calvary Baptist Church
500-516 West Sunset Drive
Rittman, Ohio 44270

Re: Dr. B. R. Lakin

The crowd overflowed the large drive-in theatre where Dr. B. R. Lakin was preaching the gospel. The man by my side was an opera singer. As we walked away after the service he said, "When he preaches, I wish that I had never committed a sin against God."

I have seen the great city crowds fill the largest auditoriums and stadiums to hear this unique man of God from the hills. And I have seen the country folk swarm down out of the hills in wagons, flat-bed trucks and by foot to sit spellbound as this great preacher made God so real, Calvary so personal and Heaven so near.

Although I am his son in the ministry, I stood as his pastor when we buried his only son high atop the West Virginia hills overlooking the peaceful valley that cradles the high log house that is home to this.giant of a preacher who for years conducted "The Nation's Family Prayer Period" from Cadle Tabernacle on WLW. Here, too, his beautiful "Miss Bob" faithfully keeps the home fires burning, the radio mail answered and the key ready to turn in the door to welcome home from his evangelistic campaigns God's great orator of the American pulpit for this generation.

H. Frank Collins D.D.
Pastor

Dr. Lakin was now able to relate by actual experience what James has so clearly stated in James 1:12; "Blessed is the man that endureth temptation; for when he is tried, he shall receive the crown of life, which the Lord hath promised to them that love him. . . ." The living, irrefutable proof of Dr. B. R. Lakin's faith lies in the fact that it has indeed been tried in the toils of adversity and has emerged as pure, shining gold from the refiner's fire.

10

"WHY GOOD PEOPLE HAVE TROUBLE"

INTRODUCTION

The perplexing question, "Why good people have trouble" has burdened the heart and troubled the minds of many good people down through the centuries. It sometimes shakes the earth under the feet of Believers like an earthquake. It dims the vision and sends the mental faculties of man reeling in quest of a logical, reasonable answer.

It is within the scope of this mystery and doubt Dr. Lakin takes up the subject, examines it in the light of God's Word and gives an honest report after proper evaluation. Every person in the world who has faced the unknown of trials in this life would greatly benefit by making a serious study of what Dr. Lakin has to say on the subject.

Dr. Lakin is not writing from hearsay knowledge or speculation. He is sharing his God-given victories over the heart-rending experiences of life. After his heart has been crushed and his eye sockets drained dry of tears, he can still say, "God loves us too much to hurt us unnecessarily and He is too wise to make any mistakes." You will doubtless be better prepared to face trials in your own life after reading what this great man of God has to say about "Why Good People Have Trouble."

Satan has always harassed Christians with this question, "WHY DO GOOD PEOPLE HAVE TROUBLE?" If the enemy of the souls of men can inject a doubt as to the wisdom of God by asking "Why?", "How?" or "When?" he will have raised a question as to His omniscience.

I wish to point out, by the use of the Scripture, that there are reasons "WHY THE RIGHTEOUS SUFFER" and that they all are a part of the beautiful scheme of God's dealing with mankind. Just as in all

things that God orders or permits, there is
design, and there is a divine reason for the
suffering of God's children.

First of all:

SUFFERING MAY BE "CHASTENING."

"For whom the Lord loveth He chaseneth,
and scourgeth every son whom He receiveth."
(Hebrews 12:6.)

Because we, as God's children are often
disobedient, we need and receive the chastening of our Heavenly Father. Chastening
may not always be in the form of physical
suffering, but often it is.

Not only is chastening of God, but it
proves our sonship. "If ye endure chastening,
God dealeth with you as sons; for what son
is he whom the father chasteneth not? But
if ye be without chastisement, whereof all
are partakers, then are ye bastards and not
sons." (Hebrews 12:7.) Not only is it God's
design that we be chastened but it is His
desire that we "endure this chastening" as
sons.

Many Christians chafe under the chastening hand of God. Satan causes them to ask,
"Why?" This "Why" reveals a lack of knowledge of our own guilt and unworthiness. For
if we would look into the black depths of
our hearts and see all of the fleshly selfish-

ness there, we would not wonder that God, through affliction, is trying to purge out the dross of our lives in the "furnace of suffering."

If we could see the end from the beginning, as God does, we would laugh through our tears to see the wonderful improvement which our Heavenly Father's chastisement works in our lives. Children never appreciate correction when they are enduring it; but in later years, when they have children of their own, they gain an appreciation of their father's chastisement, and reverence for his discipline which made for better and stronger character. "Furthermore, we have had fathers of our flesh which corrected us, and we gave them reverence; shall we not much rather be in subjection unto the Father of spirits and live?" (Hebrews 12:9.)

We would do well to recognize affliction as often being the chastisement of the Lord and make the days of quiet suffering a time for spiritual introspection and inventory.

There is a story of a highland shepherd who grew weary of the "bell sheep" leading the flock into dangerous and precipitous slopes. One day, in desperation, he deliberately broke the sheep's leg and after it healed, it had learned its lesson. It never walked in

forbidden paths again. Sickness and affliction have often been the processes whereby
the Good Shepherd has made His sheep
better. As the musician tightens the strings
on his violin almost to the breaking point,
that he might attune them to the harmonies
of the infinite, so God, through affliction,
tunes His children to Himself that they might
sing to the praise of His glory.

Remember that God's chasening is in love
and for your profit. ". . . But He for our
profit, that we might be partakers of His
holiness." (Hebrews 12:10.)

David said, "Thy rod and Thy staff, they
comfort me." It is generally known that the
"staff" was used by the shepherd to keep
the sheep from getting in "forbidden paths,"
but the "rod" was used to whip the sheep
when he wandered away. David, wisely,
found comfort in both the staff and the rod.
Chastisement in the life of a growing child
is just as essential to the development of his
character as precept. It is the way we learn
that it "does not pay to do wrong."

So, chastisement, whether in the form of
affliction or anguish in another form, is all
in the divine process and is intended for
our profit and good. Just as the husbandman
cuts back the vines that they might produce

better, the Good Husbandman of the skies often lets the knife of affliction fall upon us that we might bear more abundant fruits of righteousness.

II. SOMETIMES SUFFERING COMES AS A MINISTRY.

"But the God of all grace, who hath called us unto His eternal glory by Christ Jesus, after that ye have suffered awhile, make you perfect, stablish, strengthen, settle you." (I Peter 5:10.)

Job was called to a ministry of suffering and his patience in affliction made him an example that has survived the centuries. The world, with its material philosophy, reasons that Christians serve God with an ulterior motive. Job's accusers said, in effect, "Sure, you serve God! Look at your broad acres of rich soil and your fat herds of cattle and your stout houses and barns. Doth Job serve God for naught?"

But God had called Job to a ministry of suffering and He permitted Satan to take everything away from him except his life. "And the Lord said unto Satan, Behold all that he hath is in thy power; only upon himself (his life) put not forth thy hand." (Job 1:12.)

Satan took Job's cattle, his herds of sheep, his servants, his children and his houses but Job arose and said, "The Lord hath given and the Lord hath taken away; blessed be the name of the Lord."

Satan approached the Lord again and said, All that a man hath he will give for his life. But put forth Thy hand now, and touch his bone and his flesh and he will curse Thee to Thy face." (Job 2:5.) Satan then afflicted Job with boils from the crown of his head to the sole of his feet and he took a potsherd to scrape himself withal, and he sat down among the ashes, but the record says, "In all this did not Job sin with his lips."

Job was a minister of suffering and his patience in affliction was a greater sermon to the gainsayers of his day than the eloquence of the ancient prophets. A broken vial of perfume produces more frangrance than a whole one. Sometimes our lives, like the alabaster box, must be shattered by affliction so the beauty of Jesus may be seen in us.

Fanny Crosby lost her eyesight at an early age. Instead of being cynical about her seeming misfortune, she lifted her heart like a nightingale in the gloom of her darkness and sang the hymns that have made her name

immortal. She was called to a ministry of
suffering and responded to the divine call and
became a minister of joyfulness to untold
millions.

There was found in an African mine the
most magnificent diamond in the history
of the world. It was presented to the King
of England to shine in the crown of state.
It was sent to Amsterdam, the diamond
center of the world to be cut. The greatest
lapidary of them all was called in to cut
the gem and what do you suppose he did
with it? He cut a notch in it; then, taking a
chisel, he struck it a mighty blow and it fell
into two pieces. "What carelessness!" you
say; but not so. For weeks this particular
blow had been studied and planned. Charts
had been made of the diamond and experts
had discussed how best to cut it to advantage.
It was not a mistake; it was a crowning
achievement of the diamond-cutting art, for
the two gems which were cut from the rough
diamond are today the pride of the Queen
of England and the marvel of the world of
jewels.

Perhaps God has allowed a crushing blow
to fall upon your life. It may seem, for the
moment, to be an appalling mistake. But it
isn't. You are "in His hand," and no man

can take you out. In His infinite wisdom
and love He may allow you to suffer for a
season but He will bring you out as gold
"tried by the fire."

More eloquent than the ministry of preaching, singing or teaching is the ministry of
suffering. If you are in the "furnace of
affliction" remember, you should rejoice
that He considered you strong enough to
endure such a difficult ministry and serve
Him faithfully.

III. SUFFERING IS SOMETIMES TEST-ING.

"And He said unto me, My grace is sufficient for thee; for my strength is made
perfect in weakness. Most gladly, therefore,
will I rather glory in my infirmities, that
the power of Christ may rest upon me." (II
Corinthians 12:10.)

Affliction is a moral gymnasium where
God's children are conditioned for the "race
of life." Paul, the wise apostle, gloried in his
infirmities for by them his strength was
made perfect.

Jeremiah wrote of this great truth when
he said, "Then I went down to the potter's
house and, behold, he wrought a work on
the wheels. And the vessel that he made of

clay was marred in the hands of the potter; so he made it again another vessel, as seemed good to the potter to make it." (Jeremiah 18:3, 4.)

God ofttimes through affliction, molds, shapes and breaks our lives, and from the shapeless mass the worthless clay is fashioned into a thing of usefulness and beauty. Most of the great men of the centuries were refined and tested in the furnace of affliction.

Paul and Silas, with their backs bleeding and their feet and hands in stocks, might have let that experience in Phillipi discourage them but they dared to "sing at midnight" and the greatest victory of their lives emerged from what seemed to be the greatest defeat. When "your back is against the wall" you are in an ideal position to fight back at life and the winner is the one who can take the testings of affliction gracefully, believing implicitly that "All things work together for good to them that love God."

Pearls are beautiful jewels and possess a soft, delicate beauty unsurpassed by any other gems. They are the only costly jewels that have an animal origin. The lowly oyster is the ingenius creator of this gem. A foreign particle (perhaps a sharp piece of sand) finds its ways inside the oyster shell. The oyster secretes a solution which covers the foreign particle and eventually the pearl is formed. It is the child of suffering.

Our Heavenly Father permits the foreign particle of affliction to enter our lives. His grace, being sufficient, is lavished upon us and we are actually made to "glory in our infirmities," for we know that we shall come through the experience with a new radiance to reflect His beauty.

IV. SUFFERING IS A TESTIMONY.

The Pharisees, at the sight of the sightless young man said, "Who did sin, this man or his parents?" Jesus answered, "Neither . . . but it is that the works of God might be made manifest."

Affliction gives the Christian the opportunity to make the works of God manifest. God either gives healing grace or grace to endure. In the case of the man born blind, it was the works of God manifest in the miracle of healing and God's name was glorified. But, with Paul, who suffered from a bodily infirmity, God gave him the grace of endurance, thus comprising a miracle as great as that of healing. I believe in Divine healing but I believe God often permits His children to suffer so the world may see the sweetness with which His children are able to endure their infirmities.

To an inexperienced eye, a synthetic diamond is as brilliant as the genuine. But when these two stones are placed under water, the synthetic stone loses its brilliance while the genuine gains in luster. God sometimes leads His children through the "waters of affliction" that the world may behold our brilliance in the hour of trouble.

> "Some through the water,
> Some through the flood;
> Some through the fire,
> But all through the blood.
> Some through great trial,
> But God gives a song,
> In the night seasons and
> All the day long."

Yes, the Architect of our destinies, allows nothing to come to our lives except that which is for our ultimate good and blessing.

We can never realize that we have fully seen the Lord until we behold Him in the valley of the shadow of death. It is then that we can trustfully say, "I fear no evil for Thou art with me." It is in the midst of life's storms that we hear His blessed words,

"Peace be still!" Not until we pass through some bereavement, suffering or persecution, do we fully appreciate the Divine presence which sustains, comforts and gives peace in the tempest.

Christ comes so much nearer the soul in the valley than He does on the mountain top. His presence is more keenly felt in the desert of suffering than it is in the Garden of Prosperity. It was in the Desert of Affliction that God spoke to Moses from the burning bush and caused him to make that great decision of which it has been said, "Moses, choosing rather to suffer affliction with the people of God, than to enjoy the pleasures of sin for a season." (Hebrews 11:25.)

The night seasons of suffering increase our spiritual vision and help us to see life in its true perspective. You may think you can see farther in the day time than you can at night, but you can't. At night you can see the stars and the nearest star is millions of miles away. You would do well to see a mile in the daylight. God, in His infinite wisdom knows when to draw the curtains of night over the soul, that in the gloom of affliction, our spiritual vision may be increased and the beauty of our lives enhanced.

V. SUFFERING IS PARTICIPATION WITH CHRIST.

"And if children, then heirs; heirs of God, and joint heirs with Christ; and if so be that we suffer with him, that we may be also glorified together." (Romans 8:17.)

Suffering with Christ! What a blessed privilege! The Disciples rejoiced that their sufferings for Christ's sake, identified them with the Lord. "And they departed from the presence of the council, rejoicing that they were counted worthy to suffer shame for His name." (Acts 5:41.)

Christ was a man of sorrows and acquainted with grief. If we are to be identified with Him, we must be resigned to ·suffer for and with Him. As I have said many times, on a journey we are not so much concerned with the comforts en route as we are the joys upon the arrival at our destination. This world is not our home. We are as aliens in a strange land on our journey home. Because "we are not of the world," the world hates us. They conspire to tear down our good name and thus rob Him Who saved us of glory. We should be tolerant with a world which does not and cannot understand the mysteries of the things of God. We should remember Jesus' words when He

said, "Blessed are ye, when men shall revile
you and persecute you and shall say all
manner of evil against you falsely, for my
sake." (Matthew 5:11.)

They rejoice in our afflictions and be-
grudge what little prosperity we enjoy but
thank God, Jesus said, "Rejoice and be ex-
ceedingly glad for great is your reward in
heaven." In these experiences, which may be
inclined to make us cynical, we become
participants with Christ. Christ was hated;
we are hated. Christ was smitten; we are
smitten. Christ was crucified; He said, "If
any man would come after me, let him deny
himself and take up his cross and follow me."
Christ was afflicted; we are afflicted. He
was wounded, bruised and chastised, but as
a sheep led to the slaughter, He opened not
His mouth." His retort to their mockings and
raileries was, "Father, forgive them, they
know not what they do."

If we are to participate with Christ and
be identified with Him, our reaction to
persecution, suffering and affliction will be
one of complete resignation to the will of God.

"For we which live are always delivered
unto death for Jesus' sake, that the life also
of Jesus might be made manifest in our
mortal flesh." (II Corinthians 4:11.)

Life is made more effulgent by suffering, pain and death. The singer with a broken heart sings with greater feeling and pathos than the one who has never tasted suffering.

The rose bush is "cut" in order that it may blossom more beautifully. We are persecuted, maligned and afflicted that we may be re-created in the image of Christ. Disappointment is often His appointment and "All things work together for good to them that love God."

Why do the righteous suffer? Ah, the reasons are legion. But rest assured that no heartache, disappointment or affliction ever comes to the heart of one of God's children without His order and permission.

I watched some stone workers hewing an odd shaped stone as it lay on the ground. "What are you going to do with that?" I asked. "We are cutting it here, so it will fit in up there," the worker answered, pointing to an opening high on the tower of the great building.

In our affliction down here, the Master Mason is shaping us and fashioning us, according to His omniscient design, so we will fit in up There.

God gave to Dr. and Mrs. Lakin only one son and one grandson but He blessed them with two lovely great granddaughters. These smiling little ladies will doubtless look upon the life story of their beloved "Pop-Pop" in years to come and thank God He allowed them to be a part of that great story. They will naturally appreciate grandfather's greatness and goodness more and more in days to come when they find they cannot go anywhere in this great nation that their own grandfather had not left a great imprint in the sands of time. They no doubt will thrill to the wonderful testimonies they are certain to hear of how Dr. Lakin influenced millions of lives for good and God. Who can tell but what God may choose these young ladies to be Missionaries to carry the same Gospel grandfather had faithfully proclaimed for more than fifty years to a hopeless, doomed human race.

11

GOD'S MAN STANDS STEADFAST AND UNMOVABLE

"We are troubled on every side, yet not distressed; we are perplexed but not in despair; Persecuted, but not forsaken; cast down, but not destroyed; Always bearing about in the body the dying of the Lord Jesus, that the life also of Jesus might be made manifest in our body. For we which live are alway delivered unto death for Jesus' sake, that the life also of Jesus might be made manifest in our mortal flesh. So then death worketh in us, but life in you. We having the same spirit of faith, according as it is written, I believed, and therefore have I spoken; we also believe, and therefore speak; Knowing that He which raised up the Lord Jesus shall raise up us also by Jesus, and shall present us with you. For all things are for your sakes, that the abundant grace might through the thanksgiving of many redound to the glory of God. For which cause we faint not; but though our outward man perish, yet the inward man is renewed day by day. For our light affliction, which is but for a moment, worketh for us a far more exceeding and eternal weight of glory; While we look not at the things which are seen, but at the things which are not seen; for the things which are seen are temporal; but the things which are not seen are eternal. (II Corinthians 4:8-18)

"For we know that if our earthly house of this tabernacle were dissolved, we have a building of God, an house not made with hands eternal in the heavens. For in this we groan, earnestly desiring to be clothed upon with our house which is from heaven; If so be that being clothed we shall not be found naked. For we that are in this tabernacle do groan, being burdened; not for that we would be unclothed, but clothed upon, that mortality might be swallowed up of life. Now he that

hath wrought us for the selfsame thing is
God, who also hath given unto us the earnest
of the Spirit. Therefore we are always
confident, knowing that, whilst we are at
home in the body, we are absent from the
Lord: (For we walk by faith, not by sight;)
We are confident, I say, and willing rather
to be absent from the body and to be present
with the Lord. Wherefore we labour, that,
whether present or absent, we may be accepted of Him. For we must all appear
before the judgment seat of Christ; that
everyone may receive the things done in his
body, according to that he hath done, whether
it be good or bad. Knowing therefore the
terror of the Lord, we persuade men; but we
are made manifest unto God; and I trust also
are made manifest in your consciences." II
Corinthians 5:1-11

The wise man Solomon said, "Of making
many books there is no end; and much study
is a weariness of the flesh." This book, like
all others, in circulation, must have that
concluding page which says, "The End." The
influence of a book, good or bad however,
goes on and on. One of the great saints of
the past said the most regretful fact of his
life was that he could do nothing about the
pornographic materials he had authored,

propagated and circulated prior to his conversion.

As this book goes to press Dr. Lakin is "going strong," to put it mildly. We who are close to him marvel every day at his stamina, strength and the strenuosity of his schedule. He appears to preach with the vigor, virility and vitality of a young man. Dr. Lakin has even been able to maintain a brawn physique of robusticity to this good hour. In spite of this fact, he lives daily with an awareness this old tabernacle of the flesh is very fragile and frail. He, like John Quincy Adams who was once asked how he was, immediately replied, "John Adams is fine sir, thank you, but the house he is living in is getting in extremely poor condition." Mr. Adams knew the storms of life could break in upon the old tent of clay and cause it to collapse at any time. Dr. Lakin knows this fact also. It was said of Abel, "He, being dead, yet speaketh." If Jesus tarries His coming the influence of Dr. Lakin will live on for generations to come. Not only has he been mightily used of God in bringing the lost to Christ but an untold number of pulpits are filled with men called of God and influenced by Dr. Lakin. Many would have abandoned the ship in times of great trials if it had

not been for the encouragement they received
from God's man.

Dr. Lakin is often asked when he's going
to retire. His reply is, "The Word says I'm
to occupy till Jesus comes." He interprets
that to mean he is to be steadfast, unmovable
and always abounding in the work of the
Lord. Not even his critics can question his
faithfulness in this area.

Dr. Lakin suffered a severe heart attack
in May, 1970. He spent 18 days in the
hospital at Johnson City, Tennessee. Most
of the time he was in Intensive Care. All
over the nation prayers were being offered
in his behalf. Few people thought he would
ever preach again but by the Grace of God,
in three short months he came back strong
as ever a contender for the faith and a
champion for the cause of Christ. Dr. Lakin
often refers to his departure from the realm
of time into the measureless cycles of
eternity. He never backs away from that
issue at all. It may be in a crashed jet in
some remote land. It may be on a crowded
freeway beneath a burning automobile. Dr.
Lakin say, "No matter what may be the
means or method that hour comes to me, if
you read or hear on the news that I have
died, don't you believe it. That day will be

Graduation Day and I will have just begun to live."

There is no death! The stars go down
To rise upon some other shore,
And bright in Heaven's jeweled crown
They shine for evermore.

There is no death! An angel form
Walks o'er the earth with silent tread;
He bears our best loved things away,
And then we call them "dead."

He leaves our hearts all desolate;
He plucks our fairest, sweetest flowers;
Transplanted into bliss, they now
Adorn immortal bowers.

Probably the one thing above all others Dr. Lakin is to be admired and respected for is his firm stand for his God-given convictions. In his own quaint way he says, "In all my fifty-two years of preaching, I have never dipped my colors once." Fame and fortune could have been his in far greater measure if he had been willing to be a chameleon-type preacher willing to change his colors to suit the crowd. Dr. Lakin has always been able to repel the sharp arrows of the critics and remain unshaken by their caustic charges. He can say in humorous sattire, "I've been chewed on by goats, bitten by rats, laughed at by hyenas, struck at by serpents and sprayed by skunks but none has disturbed my preaching the Gospel."

Cowboys hang up their spurs when their work is all done in the fall. Ball players hang up their gloves when they can no longer run the bases. Soldiers lay down their rifles when they can no longer march to battle. Painters clean their brushes and put them away when they can no longer hold a firm and steady grip. Preachers, too, must close their Bibles for the last time. Their voices become cracked and broken as age affects their vocal cords. Memory fails to provide the thoughts needed from the great storehouse of knowledge and experience. Eventually, the silver chord and golden pitcher of life break for preachers the same as all mankind. Someday that familiar, unique and distinct voice of Dr. B. R. Lakin will be silenced but his message will live on till Jesus comes. God, in His pre-determinate counsel, saw fit to allow that child to be born in 1901. By the Providential direction and care of God that child became a man whose steps were ordered by the Lord. The

world is a better place because Dr. Lakin
passed this way. Drunkards, gamblers,
prostitutes, thieves, murderers and vile
blasphemers will spend eternity in Heaven
because Dr. B. R. Lakin was faithful to his
calling of preaching the Gospel. He has been
saying with Paul through these many years;
"For I am not ashamed of the Gospel of
Christ; for it is the power of God unto
salvation to everyone that believeth; to the
Jew first, and also to the Greek." Romans
1:16. "And I thank Christ Jesus our Lord,
who hath enabled me for that he counted me
faithful, putting me into the ministry; . . . "
I Timothy 1:12.

Dr. Lakin is a modest man. While others
are giving their impressive reports he remains silent. When asked approximately how
many have been converted to Christ under
his ministry, his quick reply is always, "Oh,
I don't know. . . ." Others say that one
hundred thousand is a conservative figure.
The Lord is a better statistician than I. If
Jesus tarries His coming, multitudes will yet
follow this great man of God into the
Kingdom of Heaven.

An old man traveled a lone highway,
He came to the evening cold and gray—

To a chasm, vast and deep and wide,
Through which was flowing a sullen tide.

The old man crossed in the twilight dim,
But that sullen stream held no fear for him—
But he paused when he reached the other side,
And builded a bridge so vast and wide.

Good friend said a fellow traveler near
You're wasting your time now building here,
Your journey will end at the ending of day,
And you will never again pass this way;
Why pause you so long at eventide,
To build a bridge so vast and wide?

Good friend, said the old man lifting his head,
There cometh one after me, he said—
A youth who also must pass this way,
He too must cross at the ending of day.
He too must cross in the twilight dim,
Good friend, I'm just building this bridge
        for him.

Someday God will call all his ambassadors
home. In the meantime they go home one by
one as their mission is finished here in this
strange and unfriendly land. It is the hopeful
prayer of many thousands of people to whom
Dr. Lakin has been a blessing that God will

see fit to leave him here for many years yet to come. In the meantime we may rest assured Dr. Lakin will do as Stuart Hamblen suggested in his once popular and beautiful song;

"Until then, my heart will go on singing,
Until then, with joy I'll carry on
Until the day, my eyes behold that City,
Until the day, God calls me home."

Dr. Lakin, like Paul the Apostle, has kept his eye upon the goal. His vision for a long while has been focused upon that which Tennyson caught a vision of and so well described in his beautiful poem.

Sunset and evening star,
And one clear call for!
And may there be no moaning at the bar
When I put out to sea.

But such a tide as moving seems asleep,
Too full for sound and foam,
When that which drew from out the bound-
    less deep,
Turns again home,

Twilight and evening bell,
And after that the dark!
And may there be no sadness of farewell
When I embark.

For though from out our bourne of Time
    and Place,
The flood may bear me far,
I hope to see my Pilot face to face,
When I have crossed the bar.

Dr. Lakin and his grandson Ronnie by their Winnebago. This beautiful and comfortable traveling van was presented to Dr. Lakin by pastors and churches of the Baptist Bible fellowship. The presentation was made in the summer of 1972 at the Thomas Road Baptist Church in Lynchburg, Virginia where Dr. Jerry Fallwell is pastor.